Mum

MEMOIRE OF
FRANCES, LADY DOUGLAS

MEMOIRE OF FRANCES, LADY DOUGLAS

BY

LADY LOUISA STUART

edited and introduced by

JILL RUBENSTEIN

with a preface by

J. STEVEN WATSON

SCOTTISH ACADEMIC PRESS

EDINBURGH AND LONDON

Published by
Scottish Academic Press Ltd,
33 Montgomery Street
Edinburgh EH7 5JX

SBN 7073 0358 3

British Library Cataloguing in Publication Data

Stuart, *Lady* Louisa
Memoire of Frances, Lady Douglas.
1. Douglas, *Lady* Frances
I. Title II. Rubenstein, Jill
941.107'3'0924 CT828.D/

ISBN 0-7073-0358-3

Printed in Great Britain by
Clark Constable
Edinburgh, London, Melbourne

CONTENTS

LIST OF PLATES

ACKNOWLEDGEMENTS

THE editor gratefully acknowledges the opportunity to work on this book accorded her by grants-in-aid of research from the American Philosophical Society and the Charles Phelps Taft Memorial Fund and by fellowships generously awarded by the University of Edinburgh's Institute for Advanced Studies in the Humanities and the Huntington Library. Members of the staffs of the Bodleian Library, the National Library of Scotland, the Scottish Record Office, the Sheffield Central Library, and the University of Cincinnati Library have provided invaluable assistance. To Miss Catherine Armet, archivist of Lord Bute's collection at Mount Stuart, the editor owes an incalculable debt for gracious encouragement, Scottish hospitality, and, above all, a wealth of knowledge unstintingly bestowed.

Jill Rubenstein
Cincinnati, Ohio

PREFACE

LADY LOUISA STUART is probably best remembered as a friend whose taste and judgement won praise from Sir Walter Scott. Some people may have thought that this was further evidence of Sir Walter's kindness of heart. But those who read Mrs Stuart Wortley's *A Prime Minister and his Son*, when it appeared in 1925, glimpsed evidence to justify his praise. Two or three letters from Lady Louisa printed there, along with her defence of her father as George III's Prime Minister, have a distinctive flavour.

Nevertheless, even after such sips of lemon and honey few have searched *Gleanings from an Old Portfolio* for Lady Louisa's polished piece on the Duke of Argyll, or looked for letters in the Record of her Manuscripts. We knew that anecdotes in other works were derived from her but for my own part I assumed that if there had been more substantial literary works, they had perished by accident or design.

They might well have perished by design. For Lady Louisa had no wish to figure in such places as Horace Walpole's lists of "Noble Authors". She was so deeply hidden that she did not resurface even in the vignettes of Austin Dobson which are fondly concerned with half-forgotten literature and ladies of talent and title. Lady Louisa felt, as Professor Rubenstein rightly emphasises, that learned ladies should only be heard within the circle of their intimates. This was not just a prejudice derived from the proud diffidence of the Butes or a desire to distance herself from her talented Wortley Montagu grandmother who had sought publicity at any price. More probably it was her unquestioning acceptance of the stiff social code of the middle years of the eighteenth century when she was born. As an old woman in Victoria's reign, we learn, she could still hiss and threaten to scratch when any writing of hers attracted public notice.

And yet, though she might feel that aristocratic authorship was vulgar, it is clear that the origin of her friendship with Lady Frances Scott, a friendship which was the main interest of her early and middle years and the justification of the work now presented some two centuries after the events it describes, was the latter's praise of Louisa's verses: praise, let us admit, which is difficult to justify. Such verses as Professor Rubenstein now quotes in her introduction seem to me not much above the level of those to be found in many girls' albums, where pressed flowers neighbour conventional emotions. But the literary trifles clearly meant more to the young lady than one should expect if she had been as unprofessional and unambitious as she thought she was. The praise of Frances Scott (later Frances Douglas), confesses Lady Louisa,—"opened a new world to me".

Lady Louisa's feelings get cramped by verse into a conventional mould. In prose they strike freely and express an original mind. Professor Rubenstein somewhere compares her irony to that of Jane Austen. Certainly some of her observation is marked by comparable subtlety. But usually she is fiercer and more direct. She is not persuaded by her grandmother's couplet—

> "Satire should like a Polish'd Razor keen,
> Wound with a touch that's scarcely felt or seen."

After all, she had been reared in the centre of politics and she finds her way with an aristocratic self-assurance through a man's world. No-one hid things from her.—

> "My girls", said our friend Lady Charlotte Bury, "never heard of adultery in their lives". So opposite was *F.*'s training that she heard of little else.—

and though Louisa came from a happier home background than her heroine she uses no veils whether she is writing of a Duchess's dirty underclothes or a statesman's incestuous temptations.

At times I have felt inclined to compare her to Thackeray. She has his vision of that jostling, competing, finely mannered, world of dirty tricks, that Vanity Fair, which so fascinated him.

But Thackeray is always the man outside, the observer who would have liked to try his luck with Lord Steyne for Becky Sharp, but was neither cad enough nor confident enough to do more than dream of such situations. Lady Louisa is inside. Hers is a real and not imagined world. She accepts her place in it, the high born and observant old maid.

It may seem indeed peculiar to talk of novelists in connection with Lady Louisa's work. This is after all a Memoir and, on the face of it, a piece of family history. I am, all the same, reminded of a critic's assessment of Laurence Sterne's novel *The Life and Opinions of Tristram Shandy*, that it is really the life of his uncle Toby and the opinions of his father, for the hero hardly gets born before the last pages. Though Lady Louisa's book purports to be reminiscences of her best and most loved friend, written piously for the daughter of that friend, it is a feature of the work that the central character is faint compared with these that surround her in the course of the Memoir. The tribute is to a dead friend. The interest is in the world which passed before that friend's eyes, and of which she is presumed to make the same assessment as the author. Professor Rubenstein justly says that the author permits no "independent assessment of her subject; other people are judged by how they judge her . . . and reward her excellence". But this can be put another way. The dreadful Campbell sisters, the nursery staff, the rogues, the political stylists and the quick-tongued ladies of fashion are, at the end of the day, what we remember about the work. Lady *F.* is like the fictional Tristram Shandy and unlike Boswell's Johnson in that she is really just a peg on which to hang anecdotes, an excuse for delineating some curious characters; she is an excuse to put clearly before us a very personal view of the world.

This description perhaps makes the Memoir sound like a gossip sheet of the end of the eighteenth century. It certainly has some of the lure of good gossip. Lady Louisa has more descriptions in her stories than can be found in men like Glenbervie, Wraxall or others who were whispering away for posterity about this time. I enjoy the sketch of poor Miss Townshend, whose mother Lady Greenwich had led her to expect

> —"everything wearing the form of man would hereafter come and die at her feet . . ." led by the Marquis of Graham. Though she "had a very pretty face" she was "all of a heap, lumpish, bundling, and not perfectly straight", for which she vainly tried to compensate with "drawers-full of frippery on her head".—

Poor girl, no wonder that in spite of dear *F.*'s showing her kindness for the sake of her dead father she had, in the end, nothing for it but to elope and languish in County Tyrone with the blackleg (a word which at that time meant a turf-swindler), Mr Wilson. This Wilson provokes an elaborate comparison and a memory of days of powder and pomatum when going to a

> —great ball made one wish to be particularly well-dressed, and one had bespoken a first rate French hairdresser for the purpose, it would sometimes happen that after waiting the live-long evening, one beheld one's fate sealed by the apparition of a dirty ill-looking fellow not "to be touched with a pair of tongs", who announced himself as M. Blanc's assistant (or journeyman) come in his stead . . . Mr Wilson had precisely the appearance of such a person.—

Elsewhere in this little in-set tale one learns that £100 a year was the recognised maintenance for a gentlewoman about 1770.

The value of Lady Louisa's sketch is not, however, confined to curiosities or glimpses of everyday life. She has a real if small contibution to make to the background of the political history of her times. For there are always men of affairs whose careers are difficult to explain. Why, in the lifetime of Lady Frances and Lady Louisa was Charles James Fox so powerful a figure despite miscalculations which forced him into opposition for most of his life? Why in this century is there a mystique about Aneurin Bevan which seems out of proportion to what he did or bequeathed? What, in America, was the secret of the power of John C. Calhoun or of William Jennings Bryan? Perhaps one can risk the guess that future historians may puzzle their wits how to put Mr Wedgwood Benn into a proper perspective. Such men have always been difficult to evaluate because in the first place so much depended upon their powers of speech, and eloquence is subject to fashion and dries quicker than ink on the page. But even more such men escape our judgement because the charm or unpleasantness of their personality, which was so powerful in life, is likely to defy recreation in words when moods have changed.

Of such enigmatic leaders Charles Townshend is certainly one of the most noteworthy. He was born in 1725 into that great Whig family which, with the neighbouring Walpoles, had helped to make the Hanoverian succession secure. He was related to the brothers, Henry Pelham and the Duke of Newcastle. In his youth they had Royal support in using the strings of patronage and the levers of power. Though he had powerful relations he was himself a younger son and a disparaged one. He was trained for the law and entered upon that profession. But in 1747 he persuaded his parsimonious father to pay his costs in entering Parliament for Great Yarmouth.

In their biography of Charles Townshend (published 1964) Sir Lewis Namier and John Brooke explain some of the less pleasant sides of Townshend's character by examining his relations with his bullying and changeable father. Young Charles learned to turn away wrath with soft untruths or comic turns. He would abuse his mother to get father's allowance but ran to her for much needed sympathy. Even so, it is not clear even from this biography why Townshend was so flatteringly received into the House of Commons. Family connections would be enough to get a junior office in the Board of Trade and then (apparently because he was too bored to turn up at Board of Trade meetings) secure him a place in the Admiralty. But this does not explain the way he was universally acclaimed, in a short space of time, as the coming man, and after a year or two as an erratic genius.

In 1754 the establishment of the past forty years began to crack with Henry Pelham's death and the rivalry of Pitt and Fox (later to be remembered as "the elder" in each case but at this time thrusting new leaders). This breaking surface was further to be split by the war for empire (1756-63) and even more by the peace which had to be made by ministers of the new young king, George III. The period 1760-70, in contrast to the years before 1754, is one of ministerial instability. In these stirrings and strivings, Charles Townshend tried to advance himself as quickly as possible by deserting the old patrons and by using the well-known tactic of being such a nuisance in opposition that he might hope to be bought off with office.

Townshend, presumably to secure his financial and social independence of father or political friends, had married the wealthy widow Lady Dalkeith in 1755. She was born a Campbell and cousin, as well as later on the sister-in-law, of John, the third Earl of Bute who, until 1763, was George III's first minister, having in addition to his monarch's love, the votes of a solid Scottish connection in Parliament. Charles Townshend supported Bute and was in opposition after the latter's resignation in 1763. When Bute refused or was unable to play a part in the jostling of the groups, Grenville, Bedford, Rockingham and Pitt (Chatham), Townshend became known as a Pittite and as such wriggled his way into the Rockingham government in 1765. From the first he took a strong line on the American colonies and was in favour of the Stamp Act, though the administration to which he belonged repealed it. He remained as much a maverick when, in 1766, Chatham (Pitt) replaced Rockingham but kept such ministers as the Duke of Grafton and Charles Townshend. Indeed Townshend, now Chancellor of the Exchequer, attacked his colleagues openly. On the famous occasion of his "Champagne speech" (in May 1767) he came from dining with a city alderman and made an attack on the East Indian policy to which he himself had agreed that morning. It was, said Horace Walpole, a speech which "beat Lord Chatham in language, Burke in metaphors, Grenville in presumption, Rigby in impudence, himself in folly and everybody in good humour": it proved that "he was capable of being, and unfit to be, first minister". In a similar mood, Townshend threw out his famous boast that he knew of a way of raising revenue to which the colonies could not effectively object. To live up to that he had to develop, as an alternative to direct taxation, his famous customs duties. These, as much as anything, account for the loss of America.

In spite of all this, Townshend was still in high office (though perhaps about to be dropped) when suddenly in August, 1767, he died of a putrid fever leaving his private affairs in the greatest confusion and his intrigues incomplete: "the first eloquence of the world is dumb": "those volatile salts are evaporated". The secret of Townshend's success is not fully revealed. Why did no-one, not even the great Chatham, call him to order, call his bluff, in the Cabinet? How could a young drunken epileptic sweep the whole House of Commons nearer to disaster? Percy Fitzgerald's life of him (written in 1866) makes a brave and admiring attempt to recreate his personality in action but the author's idea of the political context in which it operated is so hopelessly wrong as to make it useless. At the end of their biography Namier and Brooke make some interesting suggestions. They conjecture that Charles Townshend needed the shield of mockery to hide his poverty of heart and that he turned all things into a brilliant game so that loss would be less hurtful. Yet, they see a faint glimmer of something else, something more positive in his wish to ameliorate conditions for the insane and in his "concern for the family, his own and Lady Dalkeith's". Frances Scott of the present Memoir was, of course, one of the children of Lady Dalkeith, the child above all for whom Charles, according to Lady Louisa, cared most.

Perhaps the part of this Memoir, therefore, which will appeal most to historians is its picture in the round of Charles Townshend at home. For it suggests with gentle touches what made the man so persuasive and yet so dangerous. He had, as Lady Louisa recognises without much surprise, married the widowed Lady Dalkeith for her money and to make an independent career possible for himself. Yet ironically he had married a wife whose wild Campbell temperament he could not control and of which he was, in a word, afraid. Certainly here his defence was to use mockery. He was taken on a tour round Scotland behind his new wife. In full sail she towed him along in pride of conquest while he could also be heard calling out to the uncaring east coast baillies

> —"God bless you gentlemen. Do remember I am George Prince of Denmark at least" (referring to Queen Anne's husband whom Marlborough had "found drunk, found sober, but found no sense in").

It emerges also that Charles at this time (and all others) had the wish to please. Perhaps, as Lady Louisa speculates; "the desire of playing amiable . . . might insensibly lead him to imbibe true affection". He died more contented, we may be sure, that he had secured for his wife the Barony of Greenwich. Lady Louisa does not take his frequent infidelities as signs that he had not come to have some love for his wife. The ladies in his affairs, as she coolly remarks, came more than half-way to meet him. But it was sitting at ease with the children, particularly with Lady *F.*, his stepdaughter, that Charles found the audience and the affection he desired. He explained politics and the girl read to him from books she was fast discovering. Lady Louisa skilfully shows how he protected *F.* from the withering scorn of her mother and how he encouraged the development of her talents. Equally, she shows how dangerous this could gradually become. The line between paternal and improper affection was felt by the growing girl herself. *F.* was aware of her need to escape, for his sake as well as her own. He knew this too. But he indulged in the luxury of lamenting her desertion when she went away with her brother and his young wife, even though this was his, as well as her, escape from disaster.

When Townshend died so suddenly (in his 43rd year) Lady Frances was still only 17. Though she had fled his company she obviously wanted to convey to Lady Louisa some of her stepfather's natural charm, some of his skill in exposition, and also his suicidal liking for balancing at dangerous heights. The Townshend story is a major portion of the Memoir. It helps most effectively to explain what sort of man this was and how he influenced opinion but how he destroyed his own causes. The quiet and subtle drawing of Charles Townshend is balanced by a lively caricature of his wife. Her dislike of her own first crop of children, her booming horn of a voice, and constant activity on the scandal circuit, supply comic relief to the tragedy rather as the porter is said to do in *Macbeth*.

> —"She always does and will present herself to my mind as a wicked witch" . . . though she had been—"a *fine young* woman—that epithet belonging of the right to all dukes' daughters and rich heiresses not positively ugly".—

The flight of Lady Frances from her uncomfortable home enables the mood of the narrative to change. Up in Scotland *F.* is shown as emerging from a dangerous youth to the security first of her brother Buccleuch's household, then to that of her friend Lucy Graham who had married Lord Archibald Douglas. One feels at this point how the prospect of being always the unmarried friend worried Lady Frances. But Lucy died young. She is said to have expressed her hope that Archibald and Frances would marry. So finally, with the blessing of Lucy's mother, the old Duchess of Montrose, Frances replaced Lucy and in her turn nurtured a quiverful of children and step-children. We are now in a quiet world. There are still political figures to be brought forward and they are described with skill. But it is no longer the world of excitement and conflict, the stirrings of new talent in London.

The change is perhaps symbolised in the story that Henry Dundas wished, too late, to offer for *F.*'s hand. Dundas was certainly a man on the march, with talent very different but as thrusting as that of Charles Townshend of the earlier era. Dundas had left his early patron, the Duke of Buccleuch, behind. He was to become the real minister in control of Scotland, using influence in India to benefit and to control his adherents north of the border. He had already hitched his wagon to the younger Pitt's star. He had already, also, divorced a wife. He had long known *F.* and helped her do something for the Wilsons and others. She commented, on his affectionate remarks being reported to her, that such a predilection would now prevent her asking favours of him. She was in any case committed to

Archibald Douglas. She was entering a society in which men of established position played their parts with dignity and confidence whether in Edinburgh or in the Lord Lieutenant's lodge in Dublin. It was the world of the Duke of Buccleuch and of the Duke of Portland. The interest of the story becomes divided between the squabbles of the nursery and the petulance of official correspondence and patronage.

There is one curious silence in this domestic study. Much time is spent on speculation about *F.*'s secret and innocent love for another man. Lady Louisa is perhaps thinking as she writes of her own more open but equally hopeless love for General Medows. This speculation about *F.*'s love distracts us from consideration of her day to day feelings as a wife. Moreover, it helps to put into the shade the character and intentions of Lord Archibald Douglas himself. Yet Lord Archibald's two marriages form the middle section in one of the most lurid of disputes in Scottish high life. Archibald Douglas, formerly Steuart, was from all accounts, for they confirm that of Lady Louisa, a gentle and a worthy man. But what were his origins? That was the question which all Scotland, or rather all Britain, had been asking in the 1760s. It had produced typical answers from Dr Johnson, from Boswell, and from the great judge, Lord Mansfield. Not everyone accepted the answer of the House of Lords. In the end there were those bold enough to reckon that Heaven itself had reversed the judgement of the House of Lords.

One need not speak in riddles to explain the conundrum. The Duke of Douglas in the 1740s realised that his estates would, in default of an heir, pass to the Duke of Hamilton. To this he was reconciled, even happily, most of the time. His belated marriage to a cousin, Peggy Douglas of Mains, was construed as an attempt to get his own heir, but if it was it did not succeed, and the new Duchess was to prove his opponent in most things. The Duke had a sister, Lady Jane, who was set against the Hamiltons. She secretly married an adventurer, Sir John Steuart, an elderly bankrupt who had served in the Swedish army. I think if Louisa had ever mentioned him she would have called him too "a blackleg". The Steuarts were in France in 1748 and the lady then aged about 50, when they announced unexpectedly that she had been delivered of twin boys, Archibald and Sholto. In Scotland the Duke and others had doubts about the circumstances of their birth. Lady Jane's enemies alleged that she had bought a couple of new-born French gypsies and adopted them, to spite the Hamiltons. The Duchess, however, took the part of these new nephews who at least were decently educated at Westminster School under the care of the Duke of Queensbury, though their presumed father was first on the run and then under restraint for debt. The death of young Sholto left Archibald alone in his claim.

The Duke and Duchess quarelled so violently about the boy that between them they had contrived to burn down their castle and had to move to Edinburgh. Then in 1761, the Duke died. The battle for his inheritance promptly opened. It dragged its way through the courts 1761-69, the years when Lady Frances was going through her teens in Townshend's house, and Lady Louisa was sitting at her mother's feet in the Bute house, Luton Hoo. In the end the legitimacy of Archibald Steuart was upheld. He at once inherited the estates. He was elected to the House of Commons in 1782. He was created a British Peer, Baron Douglas, in 1790.

He was, as Lady Louisa explains in this Memoir, twice married. The second marriage took place in 1783 and was to fill the major part of her dear Lady *F.*'s life. It is strange that she does not want to comment on this dramatic past in writing for one of the daughters of Lady Frances and Lord Douglas. In fact, she mentions it only once and that in an aside near the end of her story.

She is trying to account for the coldness of the Scotts (Buccleuch) and of the Campbells (Argyll) to Lady *F.* and also to her daughter Caroline for whom the memorandum is composed. Lady Betty, née Campbell, but the wife of Stuart Mackenzie, was particularly hostile. This was the Stuart Mackenzie to whom Lord Bute had left the management of his parliamentary group twenty years before. It was indeed a small world. Lady Frances had inherited a house at Petersham.

As a maiden lady she did not need it and had lent it to Lady Betty. On her marriage, her husband insisted upon recovering it for their own use. Lady Betty seemed to forget it was not her own property:

> —She complained of *A.*'s having done the most unhandsome, unjust, unheard of thing that ever came into a man's head—and then the ingratitude of it!—*He* to dislodge *them* who had been his mother's friends, aye, and his own in adversity (Mr Mackenzie was a witness on his side in the Douglas cause).—

This is Lady Louisa's only mention of the affair. She is off to discuss her unreasonable Campbell relations and to make the acute observation that though uncle Mackenzie seemed less violent than his wife, it was simply that

> —Some men make this convenient use of a foolish violent wife: a woman's prate is of no consequence, so letting her say what they could not well say themselves, they vent their wrath at second hand; and a smile or a compassionate shrug saves the dignity of manhood harmless.—

She tells us little of the married life of her heroine. One does not at first realise that the daughter Caroline for whom the Memoir was written had five full brothers and two full sisters. It is true that Lady Louisa could not know, when she wrote, of the end to the story.

It is indeed strange that Lady Louisa averts her eyes from an issue in which her dear *F.* was personally though indirectly involved. By his two wives, Lord Archibald Douglas had no less than 12 children. Four of the boys died before their father. The other four came into the title one after the other but all without having children of their own. Of the girls, only one, Jane Margaret, had issue. This was by her marriage to a junior member of the Buccleuchs. In 1837 she inherited all the Douglas estates. She had no son but four daughters. The eldest of these married the eleventh Earl of Home. In this way the property so bitterly fought for through the courts, the occasion of so much abuse, character assassination and contrivance, passed from the apparently secure twelve pronged possession of Lord Douglas, first to the Buccleuchs and then to the Homes in so short a space of time that the devout saw the dreadful hand of the Almighty moving. It is this succession, of course, which has meant that the earls of Home inherited and have preserved the Memoir written for the daughter of Lady Douglas.

Lady Frances was born to apparent security as the daughter of Lord Dalkeith: she was plunged into the hurly burly of the Townshend menage: she then became, surprisingly, a part of the process by which the Douglas claimant seemed to consolidate his place in Scotland. But we will now remember her not as a great lady but as a sensitive girl who inspired a younger literary lady to record her personal virtues. Professor Rubenstein, with the consent of Lord Home, has made available to us all a survey of a small but extremely powerful section of British society over the period of one woman's life. This survey is made for us by a pair of acute and very feminine eyes. The report is made in a style which we can join Walter Scott in admiring, for it is elegant, and mingles acute judgement with a power to amuse.

J. STEVEN WATSON

INTRODUCTION

LADY LOUISA STUART wrote the *Memoire of Frances Lady Douglas* as a tribute to a deeply beloved and lamented friend. She presented it to Caroline Scott, Frances Douglas' daughter, as the one person who could most fittingly appreciate the excellent qualities of the subject. Writing the *Memoire*, therefore, was a private act of love, of mourning, and of recovery from the pain of loss. She never intended it for public perusal, and the manuscript has remained unpublished and in private hands until now. Mrs Scott bequeathed it to the eleventh Earl of Home; the manuscript presently belongs to Baron Home of the Hirsel, with whose gracious permission it is now published. The *Memoire* chronicles the life of its subject in a style both affectionate and unsparingly honest and offers a superb view of late eighteenth and early nineteenth century aristocratic society. Lady Louisa's observations on manners, politics, and personalities are sometimes acerbic, sometimes charitable and always infused with a characteristic combination of irony and compassion.

As the eleventh and youngest child of the third Earl of Bute, briefly Prime Minister to George III, Lady Louisa endured a wretched childhood. The target of vituperative enemies who did not hesitate to besmirch his reputation with scurrilous personal attacks, Bute fell from power an angry and embittered man. He retreated to self-imposed exile in the country to botanize in splendid solitude, wrenching his family away from London to live in the depressingly lifeless magnificence of their estate at Luton Hoo. But living in a showplace held no consolation for the little girl Louisa and her early years were clouded by her father's bitternesss as well as by the contemptuous taunts of a crowd of older but duller siblings. Her letters make it clear that while she respected and dutifully loved her father, the relationship between them remained formal and distant. Having ten brothers and sisters hardly helped, as most of them were considerably older; and she felt real affection, as distinguished from dutiful regard, for only one, Caroline, later Lady Portarlington. Although she found a kindred spirit in her mother, the child early discovered her superiority to this flock of older siblings. Writing to her young protégée Louisa Clinton in 1822, Lady Louisa reflected on her own childhood in an attempt to assuage the younger woman's discontent:

> My mother I always looked up to as what she was, the first of human beings, but all the elders were in some sort *between* her and me. She had so much to do in various ways, so many calls on her attention, so many trials, so many sorrows, that she could not but leave me in a great degree to their superintendence, and now that I am fully sobered into a very just, nay, impartial degree of self-estimation, I have no scruple of telling you they did not understand me any more than Maria does you. I have lived with my superiors in intellect and character since; have done it whenever I could; God knows, I do it in my own house in the person of my own poor humble maid. I feel every day that she has far better sense than I. But *they* had not, that is the truth of it, and tho' there was much in me wanting amendment, they did not know exactly *what*, nor how to set about it.[1]

That the resentment persisted throughout her long life measures the magnitude of the childhood suffering. Writing in February 1850 to Lady Montagu, the step-daughter of Frances Douglas, to congratulate her on the birth of a granddaughter, the ninth child of her daughter Lucy and the Earl of Home, the ninety-two-year-old Lady Louisa offers conventional good wishes and then adds a telling caution:

> First let me thank you for your bit-letter and then congratulate you for the good news, all good certainly, even the black head; but the quick recovery excellent. As you say boy or girl is signified not much to any body

> but its own self and that not yet for a while. Only let us be so well satisfied with what we have got as to pray for no more, I cannot desire a dozen of any sort; for I was myself an eleventh and always heartily sorry for it, as I dare say most people were. I hope that will not be the case with Lucy's youngest, God bless it![2]

Lady Louisa Stuart led an apparently unremarkable life, seemingly notable only for its longevity; born 12 August 1757, she died 4 August 1851. Because she never sought overtly to transcend the constraints imposed upon her by period, class, and gender, the bare biographical facts fail to reflect the extraordinary talent she possessed. As the daughter of an earl, a status she respected, Lady Louisa could not actively participate in the political and intellectual life of her time without incurring social ostracism and the dreaded label of bluestocking. However, class functioned as a blessing as well as a limitation, providing the leisure to indulge her fascination with literature, politics, and foreign affairs and giving her an entrée into the realm of power, if only as an observer. While she could not, of course, sit in Parliament, she could listen to accounts of its deliberations in the drawing rooms of those who did, participating vicariously (and more intelligently than many members) in a succession of national dramas. Her enormously wide aquaintance, branching out from family and social connections, included men high in Tory councils and the foreign service. Whereas her letters to women cover a wide range of both private and public subjects, her correspondence with men seems almost intentionally designed to grant a kind of indirect access to that world of power and controversy from which she was barred by gender.

Much of Lady Louisa's unhappiness derived from "the prejudice against learned ladies" which prevailed in her own family. Although she never knew her maternal grandmother, the outrageous Lady Mary Wortley Montagu, she lived under her shadow. This unconventional and brilliant bluestocking (1689–1762) violated most of the norms of aristocratic feminine behavior by permitting her writing to be published, living abroad and apart from her husband, associating with questionable companions, and demonstrating wit and literary skill as incisive as the most accomplished man's. As the granddaughter of this extraordinary woman, Lady Louisa was forced to hide her taste for reading and to conceal her scraps of verse, both of which, when discovered, brought taunts, ridicule, and threats that pedantry would render her a social pariah like her grandmother. So she disguised evidence of intellectual aspirations, but the concealment clearly left scars. She grew up believing that intellectual life must be led in secret or, at best, in the company of only a very few confidants. This childhood repression created a lifelong fear of ridicule and its attendant shyness along with an unshakable conviction that a woman of those inclinations could not possibly be admired by men. She early adopted a stance of self-deprecation as a device for camouflage and deflection, and the pose soon became a deeply ingrained cast of mind. The personal inhibitions thus induced, reinforced by conservative ideas about the activities proper for a gentlewoman, developed into an adamant opposition to publication. Like Scott's penchant for anonymity, which she never questioned although she did not hesitate to call him to account for artistic lapses, Lady Louisa's reluctance to publish her work was a complex emotional response to psychological and social pressures. She loathed the prospect of exposing her writing to criticism, she dreaded the notoriety attendant upon publication by an aristocratic lady, and she feared the vulnerability of writing for an audience. A scrap of early undated verse, which Lady Louisa never thought well enough of to make a fair copy, vividly conveys her sense of the personal violation to which the publishing writer is susceptible:

> When first old Bards began to feel
> The sweets poetic Raptures deal
> Perceived unknown sensations rise
> And tasted inspirations joys
> The wondering world at once o'erawed
> Found utterance only to applaud—
> Or pleasure mixing with amaze

> Ownd the sweet art above their praise
> Then poets were not forced to fly
> From social scenes & publick eye
> Their gifts in solitude to hide
> And the lov'd breath of fame avoid
> [Flattery] pale nor clamour rude
> Nor keen Despight their steps pursued
> Nor durst the shafts of Ignorance
> Against their Labours e'er advance.
> In those Blest days they were not born
> To bear the pedant's haughty scorn
> To hear insipid laughs go round
> And empty arguments abound.[3]

The poetry is unpolished, but Lady Louisa's nostalgia for a lost golden age of unsullied artistic integrity is poignant. She extended this personal revulsion to friends and consistently decried publication of their efforts as well as of her own. Writing to Mrs Stewart Mackenzie in June 1816, she reinforced her advice to that lady not to publish her Indian journal:

> I do not repent of my advice to you. Have you repented of following it, or do you waver? I am more than ever confirmed that loss of caste and what is worse, loss of peace and comfort would have been the consequence. You would have had from your ~~high~~ [sic] connections high compliments in the *Edinburgh Review*, and that would have determined the other Reviews to sneer with all their might.[4]

In a period of fiercely partisan reviewing when political allegiance at least as much as literary merit determined critical assessment, Lady Louisa's point is understandable. But the choice of words indicates that snobbery rather than intellectual fastidiousness motivated the advice, and this suspicion is confirmed in a letter to Louisa Clinton of November 1833. Lamenting the anonymous publication of *Trevelyan* by Lady Caroline Scott (for whom she wrote this *Memoire*), Lady Louisa wrote: "*Trevelyan* is as much *blown*, I am afraid, as if the name were affixed to it. I say 'I am afraid,' for I will own to your private ear that I cannot get over my old—perhaps *aristocratic*—prejudices, which make it a loss of caste."[5] She used that same telling phrase—"loss of caste"—to deplore Maria Edgeworth's published fiction.

Aristocratic prejudices, disdain for criticism, and childhood terrors combined to keep most of Lady Louisa's work unpublished until well after her death; much of it remains so today. She ventured into print only once in her lifetime, in the "Introductory Anecdotes" to her nephew Lord Wharncliffe's edition of the *Letters and Works of Lady Mary Wortley Montagu* (1837). Motivated by Wharncliffe's entreaties, by the desire to make some money for another nephew who performed many of the editorial chores, and perhaps by a lingering respect for that never-known grandmother whose example caused so many of the pains of her childhood, Lady Louisa wrote the sympathetic and witty biographical sketch which was printed anonymously with the letters. When John Wilson Croker identified her as the author in the February 1837 number of the *Quarterly Review*, she could barely control her fury and uncharacteristically and impulsively considered entering the literary fray against him. The cooler heads of Wharncliffe and J. B. S. Morritt prevailed, and she expended her wrath in private letters rather than in public rebuttal. The tone of these letters, however, is startlingly intemperate, especially within the larger context of Lady Louisa's generally controlled correspondence.

While she found pleasure, then, in clandestine intellectual pursuits, the loneliness of Lady Louisa's childhood still left her starved for friendship, as the *Memoire* hints. Although her imagination initially invested Miss Townshend, Lady Frances' half-sister, with qualities which the girl clearly did not possess, it was Lady Frances Scott who was to become her first real friend and provide the most intense experience of her young life. When at the age of nine or ten she first met this sixteen-year-old cousin, she was immediately captured by the powers of mind and merriment of her newly found relation. As the two girls matured, the friendship deepened and became increasingly precious to both;

it provided the standard by which subsequent ones would be measured. As the *Memoire* indicates, Lady Frances endeared herself to the adolescent Lady Louisa by praising her poetry, a rare expression of commendation for which the younger girl thirsted. The acclaim inspired trust, and Lady Louisa accustomed herself to sharing verses with her friend, always with the caveat, however, that they were to be judged with the eye of friendship, not with the eye of the critic. In her poem "To Lady Frances Scott: *Envoi*: of some pieces in verse 1781" she clearly distinguishes between the two modes of appraisal and chooses the less risky:

> Go, idle rhymes! To friendship's hand repair
> Safe be your rest and faithful Delia's care;
> No kinder wish your parent's voice can frame:
> Go! Quiet sleep and long oblivion claim;
> Unawed by sterner glance, contented lie,
> Nor fear contempt from Delia's partial eye.
> For partial will't not be, my Delia, say?—
> —Shall critic censure here have rig'rous sway?
> No—let indifference blemishes deride,
> Thy heart shall now become thy judgement's guide
> Securing kind acceptance of the strain
> —The last, it may be, thou shalt e'er obtain—[6]

The authorial insecurity between the lines is all too obvious, but the fact remains that the poems were indeed shared (and apparently duly praised), an immense step toward the mature confidence of the woman from the pathetic vulnerability of the child.

From a miserable child, Lady Louisa grew into a more self-possessed but frequently unhappy young woman. This period of her life was spent primarily as her mother's companion; at Luton, which she continued to loathe; at Wharncliffe, Lady Bute's estate in Yorkshire where Lady Louisa first discovered her taste for wild natural beauty; at Bath, where Lady Bute went to take the waters for gout; and in London, where Lady Louisa attended all the social functions appropriate for one of her station while dutifully subduing her own inclinations to her mother's engagements and choice of associates. It was not an onerous life, and by all accounts Lady Bute did indeed prove a suitable intellectual companion to her daughter. The personal memories and stories of their youth told by Lady Bute and her friends inculcated in Lady Louisa that sense of social and historical continuity which would make her so congenial to Walter Scott when they met at Dalkeith. They also provided a rich store of anecdotes which she later employed to great advantage in the "Introductory Anecdotes" to the Wortley Montagu correspondence, in the "Notes" to Jesse's *George Selwyn and His Contemporaries*, and especially in her most polished work, the "Account of John, Duke of Argyll, and His Family". The latter two pieces remained unpublished during Lady Louisa's lifetime but have since been printed. Social be-behavior fascinated the observant young woman, whose letters to her married sister Caroline are replete with unapologetic gossip and tales of who went where with whom. However, although a willing participant in the routs, balls, card parties, morning visits, and excursions to the opera which these letters describe, she almost always maintained an ironic distance in the telling which became more pronounced as she grew older. Some of the letters of this period are miniature Austenian gems, written (and probably rewritten) for the delectation of Lady Louisa's sister in Ireland and especially for the Douglas and Buccleuch circles in Scotland. The irony is never malicious, and the writer's sense of superiority remains carefully submerged, while her delight in the ridiculous exhilarates the prose. Writing to the Duchess of Buccleuch in November 1785 from Bath, where she had obediently accompanied her mother, Lady Louisa sets a scene worthy of Smollett:

> Here are the abundance of Irish *Quality* & *Gentry*, & a great collection of boys of eighteen. Her Grace of Athol & family head the balls as it is their right to do. One of her girls seems pretty. She herself is a sight to be seen: she has shaved her head, I believe, bound it tight in a black hood & reduced it into a smaller compass than ever head was before: the rest of her dress is (to treat Lady F. & you with a vulgar expression) *black and all black*; black up

> to the chin, & black down to the fingers' ends. She means, I suppose, to pass for an old Nun, but I don't know how it is, she looks much more like an old Fryar. And somebody said they were sure there was no more clean Linen out of sight than there was in it. . . . I have just been present at the election of a Master of the Ceremonies for the lower Rooms, the best burlesque upon other elections that can be conceived & the most admirable scene I ever saw. The tattling & giggling of us Ladies, the important gravity of some of the men, the serious forms of moving, seconding, opposing the motion, humbly conceiving, the respect due to this assembly, the occasion wherefore we are called together etc. etc. together with "Ladies & Gentlemen! I do beseech you, one at once"— "Nay, but dear Sir! I can't hear a word you say"— "Madam, be pleased to be silent one minute"—"Stay! stop! what, are you all running away before the business is half over?" & At last the Chairman's putting *the Question*—Is it your pleasure that Captain King be elected your Member of—pook! pshaw! Your Master of the Ceremonies—All this had an effect more ridiculous than can be described.[7]

In spite of the jollity of letters such as this, the young woman continued to suffer from a tendency toward depression, perhaps the remnant of that romantic melancholy she so self-consciously cultivated as a girl. In a poem written in 1778 or 1779 to Lady Caroline Dawson, the recently married sister whom she missed terribly, Lady Louisa analyzed her unhappiness and indulged in a rare moment of self-pity:

> If bliss from worth, if strength from firmness flow,
> Such is the fate thy patience sure shall know.
> Far diff'rent mine—Each bud of seeming joy
> The gloomy Presage can betimes annoy,
> Deep to my bosom's inmost folds proceed,
> Pluck the weak root, and bruise the little seed,
> Or if the transient bloom ere then be fled,

Pour fost'ring drops on sorrow's hateful head,
And lest some ray of adverse sun impair,
Shade the night plant with unabating care.[8]

Lady Louisa was to wage a lifelong Johnsonian struggle against this inclination to reject happiness; the effort was generally successful, but even in old age her psychological equilibrium required constant vigilance to maintain. Ill fortune in love exacerbated the problem. Her only real attachment, to William Medows, a kinsman and a younger son, was forbidden by Lord Bute, and the resultant pain lingered long. The experience of real love determined her to accept nothing less genuine. Subsequent suitors included Henry Dundas (later Lord Melville), who, according to the *Memoire*, confessed to an earlier passion for Lady Frances herself, and John Charles Villiers; but they had to contend with Lady Louisa's memory of Medows and so met with no encouragement. "Fye upon Cupid," she wrote in 1785, "the nasty little devil has used me always ill, and now if he chose to present me with one of that set of company, he might have shot to better purpose."[9] She early accustomed herself to old maid status and referred to it easily and with engaging self-mockery. In 1800 she invoked it to justify forgoing a legacy from an uncle in favor of her sister's children, and one of her most remarkable letters, written at the age of ninety-two to Sophia, wife of the second Marquess of Bute, described her seal (an owl perched on a teapot over the motto from *The Rape of the Lock* "Sometimes Counsel, Sometimes Tea") as "the *arms* of an *old maid*".[10] That Cupid used her ill, however, never embittered Lady Louisa on the subject of love, as her comments in the *Memoire* on Lady Caroline Scott's marriage clearly indicate. The sensitive treatment of the scars left upon Lady Frances' mind by an impossible and unrequited love reflects, perhaps, the author's own triumph of will in an analogous situation.

Lady Frances Scott was born in 1750, the posthumous child of the Earl of Dalkeith and Lady Caroline Campbell. Had her father lived, he would have been Duke of Buccleuch, and so the title passed to her brother. Her mother was the eldest of four daughters of the second Duke of Argyll, the band of sisters which Lady Louisa calls "the Waywards". One of them, Lady Mary Coke, appears in the Walpole correspondence and is the subject of a devastatingly funny memoir by Lady Louisa Stuart. Through their common descent from Archibald, first Duke of Argyll, the Campbell sisters were cousins of Lord Bute, Lady Louisa's father, and so Lady Louisa and Lady Frances were also cousins. Caroline Campbell was a spoiled and imperious girl whose first marriage improved her character not at all. According to Lady Louisa, she detested her daughter and derived perverse pleasure from making her life as miserable as possible. When Frances was five, her mother married Charles Townshend, the brilliant, mercurial leader of the House of Commons, known equally for his wit, his oratory, and his wildness. One of his last acts before dying at forty-two was to have his wife created Baroness Greenwich. Wedded to a termagant, Townshend took refuge at home in cultivating the affections and intelligence of his little stepdaughter, who received from him eagerly the first love she had ever been offered. Lady Louisa treats this complex relationship with great insight and a delicate balance of tact and candor.

Rescued from this increasingly precarious situation by the return of her brother from abroad and his subsequent marriage, Lady Frances accompanied her brother and sister-in-law to Scotland in the summer of 1767. There she met Archibald Lord Douglas, who would marry Lady Frances' close friend Lucy Graham four years later. Lady Lucy died in 1780, and in May 1783 Lady Frances Scott became the second wife of Archibald Douglas. Lady Louisa Stuart travelled to Scotland with the newly married couple that summer, and the journey offered her first real taste of freedom. Her letters vividly convey strong feelings of release, intellectual engagement, delight in relative independence and in the welcome variety of new people, scenes, and experiences. She revelled in the beauty of Bothwell, in the colorful tales of what Lady Frances described as "antediluvian Douglasses", and of course in the scenery. She made the acquaintance of Scottish relations and, more memorably, of the intellectual luminaries of Edinburgh, then flourishing as the

Athens of the North. A lively letter from Lady Frances to Lady Bute affectionately mocks her friend's fascination with the conversation of Principal Robertson and Lord Monboddo, but behind the burlesque lies a sort of wonder at the blossoming of the younger woman. This visit proved to be the first of many; the happiest moments of Lady Louisa's life would be spent at Bothwell and Dalkeith, where she made almost annual visits after the death of her mother in 1794.

This loss required an immensely difficult adjustment. As the companion of Lady Bute's later years and the only one of her eleven children to share her tastes and interests, Lady Louisa mourned her mother with an intensity which apparently startled some of her siblings. The letters among them shortly after Lady Bute's death imply that she was for some time quite frantic with grief. The depth of her love for her mother may be inferred from those passages in the *Memoire* which describe the relationship between Lady Greenwich and her daughter Frances. Although Lady Louisa grew up knowing that no affection subsisted between them, she found the awareness difficult to assimilate, and suppressed incredulity permeates the assurances that this relationship was taken for granted by all concerned. After the first acute grief at the loss of Lady Bute dissipated, and the solicitude of brothers and sisters diminished or disappeared altogether, Lady Louisa found both affliction and consolation in her new life. The transition from daughter of an earl's household to maiden lady of limited means required humility and forbearance. Writing many years later in February 1836 to her niece Louisa Bromley, Lady Louisa expressed sympathy for a mutual acquaintance who had lost her father the previous summer:

> I have a great liking for her, besides entering into her situation more than people can do who have never known what the breaking up of a family is, and how different in all respects the state of the solitary old maid to that of the daughter of people of any consideration in the world—how deference, and court, & flattery, and

> acquaintanceships, aye & sometimes what have been taken for friendships, march off along with the rest of the establishment, and you wake as if out of a dream.[11]

As time assuaged grief, Lady Louisa Stuart set about rendering "the state of the solitary old maid" as comfortable as possible. She discovered the pleasure of traveling where and when she would, choosing her own companions, setting her own engagements, indulging and expanding her many interests. She surrounded herself with friends and relations and, until deafness precluded conversation in extreme age, rarely wanted for company. She led a quiet but busy life, maintaining an extensive correspondence, managing her own domestic and financial affairs and helping with those of her sisters when they became incompetent, paying a regular round of long country house visits, and writing, but only for the eyes of closest friends. She read omnivorously, favoring biography and fiction but also keeping current in both the Whig and Tory periodical press. Always conscious of the strictures of class and gender and their attendant limitations, she scrupulously observed the proprieties and criticized those who did not. Her detestation of the meddlesome "female politician" appears in the *Memoire* in the caricature of Lady Greenwich on her daily rounds as "the Morning Post". A woman of strong and consistently Tory political convictions, Lady Louisa refrained from expressing them in general company as a breach of decorum and of course would not consider entering the fray of periodical publication. When Lord Brougham, the former Whig Lord Chancellor, attacked her father's reputation in the *Edinburgh Review* (July 1838), she rose to his defense by forcing Brougham to revise his view of the former Prime Minister, but only indirectly, through the mediation of her nephew, the diplomat Lord Stuart de Rothesay. Old-fashioned scruples prevented her from communicating directly with Brougham or permitting him to cite her as his source of information.

As a writer Lady Louisa Stuart excelled in what were perhaps the two most characteristic genres of her time, the familiar letter and the informal memoir. Letters provided a substitute for the public intellectual discussion in which she could not participate. In them she freely expressed a wide range of literary judgments. Sir Walter Scott considered her a superb critic, and her letters to him are among the most thoughtful and judicious he received. He collaborated with her on the unfinished "Private Letters of the Seventeenth Century" and commended her rare combination of literary acuity and tact to an aspiring writer:

> If you turn your thoughts to Belles Lettres, the best critick I know would be Lady Louisa Stuart, indeed I do not know a person who has the half of her taste & talents or could do a young author half so much good. Lady Louisa unites what are rarely found together, a perfect tact such as few even in the highest classes attain with an uncommon portion of that rare quality which is called genius.[12]

Lady Louisa's letters also provided a forum for the expression of political opinions and the analysis of national and international affairs. Although she necessarily acquired her information from either reading or hearsay, she managed to remain remarkably well informed, thanks in part to social and family connections. She assiduously cultivated the friendship of intelligent men such as J. B. S. Morritt and her favourite nephew Lord Stuart de Rothesay who were willing to indulge her taste for long letters about public events and who provided a knowledgeable and cosmopolitan point of view. Had she been interested in critical acclaim, this fascination with the world might have made Lady Louisa Stuart one of the most accomplished memoir writers of her time. The Argyll memoir, which she circulated in manuscript among a few intimates, is brilliant indeed, worthy of Walpole at his best. The "Notes" to Jesse's *Selwyn*, while less polished, sparkle with the same wit and bemused fascination with the vagaries of men and women in society. These remained in manuscript until W. S. Lewis edited them in 1928. Both works reflect Lady Louisa's fundamental belief that intellectual and spiritual health depend upon a reaching outward from the self toward and beyond one's own time and place, a belief which also infuses her letters and the conduct of her life.

This openness to experience endowed Lady Louisa with a great natural talent for friendship, which filled the voids in her life left by circumstances. Her affections were selective but intense, and, once established, her loyalty never wavered. Notwithstanding a plethora of relatives, Lady Louisa considered friendships stronger than family ties, and the relationships which meant most to her were the ones she chose. Writing in 1838 on the death of Lady Caroline Scott's closest friend, Lady Louisa made a rare confession: "Some people have no notion of attachment out of their own family, *I* have, because, God knows, it has been my lot to lose friends who were dearer to my heart than any of my brothers or sisters."[13] Because she lived to such a great age, Lady Louisa repeatedly suffered the death of friends, and some of her most poignant letters concern these losses. She compensated by establishing friendships which spanned generations, forging deep and intimate ties with the daughters of her own contemporaries and with several nephews and nieces. In some of these young men and women she took an interest much stronger than one would expect from an aunt, and they responded by becoming worthy intellectual and emotional confidants. Perhaps the most moving testimony to her capacity for friendship came from Sir Walter Scott, writing *de profundis* in February 1826 just after his bankruptcy:

> God bless you my Lady Louisa. You have been since I knew [you] the ready and active comforter of much distress indeed I think that things have happened to exercize your feelings in the behalf of others merely because you really have that sincere interest in the griefs of others which so many people make the ostensible show of—[14]

The friendship with Lady Frances Scott offered a model for those which followed. The two young women quickly discovered themselves to be kindred spirits, loving the same things, people, and places, and endowed with strikingly similar abilities.

Lady Louisa's narratives of the time spent at Bothwell comprise her happiest letters, and it was there or elsewhere in the company of Lady Frances that she wrote her liveliest poems: "Black Monday at the Royal Oak", "Tiny's Sabbath", "The Cinder King", and "Ugly Meg", the mock Border ballad which so intrigued Scott. Jane Douglas' account of their jaunt to the Lakes in 1880 and of the hilarity in which they indulged (published in *Gleanings From an Old Portfolio*) conveys the buoyant cross fertilization of wit which occurred between these two remarkable women. A poem written during that first visit to Scotland, immature and formulaic as it is, nevertheless exudes a sense of the joy they derived from each other's companionship. Lady Louisa annotates the poem in her fair copy as having been "Written upon the request of Lady Frances Douglas to have some lines dated from her house to recall the time we had passed together."

Bothwell Castle fourth of October 1783

View here the Date thou wishest to behold;
Now ripe to gladden nor to pain thine eye;
'Till o'er us both full many a sun has roll'd
Its secret vitue shall unwakened lie.

But when these hours of mutual comfort rest
Beneath the pressure of Time's aweful seal;
When weak and wav'ring mem'ry can at best
But pourtray half that now we think and feel;

Turn to this page, as near the rushing Clyde
Some smiling eve of summer thou shalt stray,
As thou shalt view yon fabric's hoary pride,
Turn to this page, my friend, and turning say

—"The maid who loved me, she was then my guest;
"Fond of these haunts she with me wandered here,
"My musings shared, my infant train carest
"And left my threshold with regret sincere"—

'Though fortune fail to change; 'though kind as now,
She thee nor me of one delight bereave,
A sigh which reason may not dare avow
Involuntary sadness than shall heave;

Then will each little moment's speech or deed
Rush on thy mind and in thy bosom swell,
And fancy, eager on the past to feed,
Feel all the magic of the latent spell.[15]

Lady Louisa never returned to Bothwell after Frances Douglas died in March 1817; the thought of it evoked only sad memories and a desire to avoid the once loved place. The pain dissipated very slowly. In 1824 she offered to send to Jane Douglas (now Lady Montagu) a memento of that happy time, and the distress is still quite evident, seven years later:

> I always meant to *leave* it you—a little book that both you & Car helped to embellish—all the nonsense of the year 1800 collected—On trying to look it over, I find the many little things which are most closely connected with whatever was then said & done, the jokes of the day & hour, only awaken pain. . . . To you it will just recall your blossoming days. . . . So *just say* whether I shall send it, or whether you shrink from the thoughts of seeing it again as yet, & would rather it staid with me while I stay?—You probably recollect the little volume I mean, with "Folies du Nord" in Gothic letters of your own tracing—[16]

The halycon days at Bothwell ended abruptly, and the depth of Lady Louisa's grief may only be inferred, as she was always reluctant to anatomize her own feelings. However, her vulnerability may be imagined from the circumstances of her life at this time. She always believed that women feel bereavement more deeply than men because they lack other outlets for their emotions. And at this point in her life religious consolation was unavailable. Lady Louisa's Christianity was confined primarily to superficial observance; even in old age, when she conscientiously struggled to attain a more profound faith, she could never quite manage to believe in an afterlife. Always hesitant to proffer to others what she contemptuously labeled "the common topics of consolation", she recognized the utility of Christian convictions at a time of bereavement but felt incapable of grasping them for herself. As late as 1839 at the age of eighty-one, writing to a younger friend on the death of her father-in-law, Lady Louisa acknowledged that "real consolation" can come only "from a higher source", and that "Otherwise time alone must weaken the sense of the deprivation".[17]

She did manage to find some consolation in expressing her feelings to a few people, but only after considerable time had passed. Her first letter on the subject seems to have been written to Jane Montagu almost three months after the event. Coming from a woman habitually reticent about her own emotions, the letter is particularly affecting in its fluent description of bereavement and of her inability to assimilate the actuality of loss:

> . . . when one has come to one's senses after the first dreadful shake, when people have done being anxious about one & half expect one to be comforted, then comes the recoil of the blow, then the full entire sense of what has happened presses on one's heart with a weight that appears to increase & sink one lower & lower every day—I was precisely in your case myself—to be sure very differently circumstanced in one respect, because *I* might reasonably think it an equal chance that I should be taken first; but it was not a thing I had ever looked forward to, and the suddenness of the deprivation brings on sometimes a sort of insane doubt whether it be really so—ten times a day I am near starting up from the wounds my own mind gives me, just as a stranger ignorant of the fact might do in talking—involuntarily I think, "I will write this, I will tell that"—but I do wrong to dwell on such things.[18]

Sir Walter Scott had also been very fond of Lady Douglas and was closely connected with the friendship between the two women.

Lady Louisa could not bring herself to write to him until fully nine months after Lady Douglas died, and there is a telling hiatus in their correspondence between 10 February 1817 and 2 January 1818, when she sent him a brief note of thanks for the receipt of *Rob Roy*. By the end of that month, however, she was finally ready to pour forth her feelings and wrote her most moving eulogy of Lady Douglas in a letter to Scott of 27 January 1818:

> Indeed, indeed, such a character is produced but once in a century or two, & vainly may we look round for her like now on earth. Madame de Sevigné did not stand more alone in her age and country. There were some points of resemblance between them, the ease, the nature, the unconsciousness of superiority, the exquisite feeling of all that struck them as excellent in others, of virtue, of generosity of mind, of genius, of wit & humour; but *her* understanding & judgement were of a stronger sort than Madame de Sevigné's, & her freedom from prejudices of every kind consequently greater. There lay the wonder; with that strong clear sense, were united the simplicity & humility which we know to have been meant when it was said of children "*Of such is the kingdom of Heaven*"—[19]

In the same letter she suggested to Scott that he might memorialize Lady Douglas, not in an epitaph or monody, which are "made by every body upon every body", but in a fictional character which would capture "the peculiar *raciness* there was *there*". That Scott adopted the suggestion is doubtful, but Lady Louisa, seeking comfort wherever she might find it, convinced herself that he modeled Jeanie Deans upon the memory of Frances Douglas. Although she directly questioned him on the subject, Scott tactfully declined to answer her query, and Lady Louisa had to remain content with speculation.

The *Memoire of Frances, Lady Douglas* is, of course, a memorial as well as a memoir. Written for the daughter of her dead friend, it exemplifies Lady Louisa Stuart's profound conviction of the importance of memory across generations. Like Scott, she regarded time and history, especially personal history, as a vital, living continuum, and this belief was responsible for her fascination with genealogy, demonstrated partially in the Selwyn "Notes" and most remarkably in the correspondence with her nephews in preparation of the Wortley Montagu letters. She served as a peerless research assistant, relying on her extraordinary memory of Lady Bute's conversation to provide information which considerably antedated her own span of recollection. In an 1829 letter to Lady Montagu she promised her a copy of Lady Douglas' version of "Cinderella" and expressed great pleasure that the Montagu children took an interest in their mother's past.[20] Given this sense of personalized history, it was therefore natural that Lady Louisa should write the *Memoire* for Lady Caroline Scott, to whom she also addressed the Argyll memoir. However, this effort constituted only one, albeit the most heartfelt, of several gestures of commemoration undertaken as the pain of loss became gradually tolerable. In 1824 she sent the Bothwell book to Lady Montagu. At some time probably in the early 1820s she undertook the "explanatory notes to the letters written by Ly. F. Scott, to the Dss. of Buccleuch from Ireland in the year 1782".[21] The manuscript is not dated, but internal evidence suggests this period. She completed the final draft of the Argyll memoir in March 1827; it is a considerably more polished literary effort than this *Memoire*, which was probably composed a few years earlier. None of her letters refers to it directly, and it is impossible to determine how long Lady Louisa took to write it.

Nevertheless, we can speculate with some certainty on why she wrote it. In addition to its announced function as family history, the *Memoire* serves its author as an elegy should, providing a vehicle for the formal resolution of grief and the final acceptance of loss. After the 1820s, therefore, Lady Louisa's letters hardly ever allude to Lady Douglas. The obeisance has been paid, the revered friend has been appropriately memorialized, and the obsessive mourning may cease. Writing the *Memoire*, then, was both an act of purgation and an act of piety.

As such, of course, it does not offer an objective assessment of its subject's character, and Lady Louisa is less than candid about Lady Douglas' shortcomings, even the ones she incidentally acknowledges elsewhere, such as a tendency toward extreme nervousness and hysterics, noted occasionally in early letters. In the *Memoire* other women consistently appear to disadvantage in contrast to Lady Douglas: Lady Greenwich; Miss Townshend; Lady Mary Coke; Lady Betty Mackenzie (another aunt); "Mum", tyrant of the Bothwell nursery; even the Duchess of Buccleuch—all display flaws of character, to a greater or lesser degree, which are set off against one or more of Lady Frances' merits. She and by implication the author appear to be the only admirable women directly present. Lady Louisa permits no independent assessment of her subject; other people are judged by how they judge her and the extent to which they recognize and reward her excellence. Thus Charles Townshend, the Duchess of Montrose, and Archibald Douglas are all presented as exemplary because they loved and trusted Lady Frances. This standard of measuring character subtly benefits and reinforces the authorial voice; as we are told repeatedly to respect and trust those who loved Lady Frances, we find ourselves respecting and trusting the author, and the device becomes a cleverly self-fulfilling moral test to establish authorial credibility. The openly avowed, intimate relationship between the author and her subject precludes the possibility that the *Memoire* could achieve the high level of biographical excellence which Lady Louisa attained in the Argyll memoir. However interesting her character, Lady Douglas remains always a focus of *personal* admiration and emotion and thus fails to become an individual of potential moral significance to all readers.

However, the critic must remember that this is a memoir and not a life and makes no pretence to either documentation or objectivity . The first few sentences candidly and cleverly avow that it is a work based on memory, prejudice, and subjective assessment, and the disclaimer forewarns the reader not to expect impartial evaluations. Indeed, the *Memoire* gains its vitality from precisely this subjective quality, which vivifies and enhances what might be dispassionately regarded as an unremarkable life transformed by a remarkable writer. Lady Louisa's narrative skill and obvious sincerity allow our sympathies to become deeply engaged; she possesses in abundance that quality which Carlyle identified as the key to the biographer's craft:

> One grand invaluable secret there is, however, which includes all the rest, and, what is comfortable, lies clearly in every man's power: *To have an open loving heart, and what follows from the possession of such*! Truly has it been said, emphatically in these days ought it to be repeated: A loving Heart is the beginning of all Knowledge. That it is that opens the whole mind, quickens every faculty of the intellect to do its fit work, that of *knowing*; and therefrom, by sure consequence, of *vividly uttering forth*. Other secret for being "graphic" is there none, worth having: but this is an all-sufficient one.[22]

The presence of the authorial voice is subdued; it remains always in the background, never blocking the reader's view of the subject. Nevertheless, the author's values emerge quite clearly; she esteems in Lady Douglas qualities of discretion, emotional discipline, sensitivity to feelings, openness to experience, and loyalty to family, even where that loyalty is clearly unmerited. Her virtues are the social virtues—friendship and the domestic affections; we are told only a little about her intellectual life and nothing of her spiritual life, reflecting Lady Louisa's almost wholly secular cast of mind. The author addresses her reader as a friend and assumes common values and judgements, a perfectly acceptable stance in a work written for the private perusal of a single known reader. Lady Louisa makes a few perfunctory gestures toward decorum amd family loyalty; Lady Greenwich was, after all, Mrs Scott's grandmother, and Lady Betty Mackenzie and Lady Mary Coke her great aunts. In general, however, the author assumes the liberty contingent on shared opinions of these people and on her own family connections; that Lady Louisa is also related to most of those she so cleverly devastates gives her a sort of freedom which could not properly be taken by an outsider.

Notwithstanding the author's declaration, however, it is difficult to believe that the *Memoire* was intended, consciously or otherwise, for the eyes of only Caroline Scott. Lady Louisa does indeed make frequent references to Mrs Scott's special concern and to her span of personal memory, but she also includes details, sometimes accompanied by rather lame excuses, that this particular reader would not require; one can assume, for example, that she knew what her own mother looked like and that she was acquainted with the fate of Mr Townshend's two sons. The author appears constantly cognizant of the presence of her un-unknown readers, and she possesses a sure sense of what will appeal to them: the mildly titillating hints of incestuous desires and unrequited love; the unjust persecution of chilhood innocence; the ugly duckling daughter, destined to be an old maid, emerging into a swan as the mistress of a great house; the hereditary streak of insanity in an ancient and powerful family; the subplot of the prodigal daughter eloping with an Irish fortune hunter; glimpses of the domestic manners and tribulations of high life; and the merest hint of a superior woman subduing her native wit and intellect to please an inferior husband. Lady Louisa Stuart owned an unfailing instinct for capturing the attention and sympathy of a reader, and that instinct molded the shape of this *Memoire* as surely as its author's more conscious motives. More than a century and a half have passed since its composition, but the *Memoire* remains an engaging and artful testament to the surpassing power of friendship. As such, one cannot suppose even Lady Louisa Stuart would object to its publication now; indeed, she might just have harbored a secret joy in the event.

JILL RUBENSTEIN
University of Cincinnati

NOTES

1. Letter to Louisa Clinton, [August 1822], *Letters of Lady Louisa Stuart to Miss Louisa Clinton*, ed. James A. Home (Edinburgh: David Douglas, 1901-1903), I, 265.
2. Typed transcript of letter to Lady Montagu, 26 February 1850, Douglas Home papers, Scottish Record Office (S.R.O.) ref. TD.80/33, box 104/3, fol. 135.
3. Bodleian MS. Eng. misc. b.164, fol. 21.
4. Transcript of letter to Mrs Stewart Mackenzie, [June 1816], Douglas Home papers, S.R.O. ref. TD.80/33, box 105/3, fols. 1-2.
5. Letter to Louisa Clinton, 18 November 1833, Clinton letters, II, 407.
6. Bodleian Ms. Eng. poet. d.202, fol. 7.
7. Letter to the Duchess of Buccleuch, 5 November 1785, Douglas Home papers, S.R.O. ref. TD.80/33, box 190, bundle 6, letter 9.
8. *Gleanings From an Old Portfolio*, ed. Mrs Godfrey Clark (Edinburgh: David Douglas, 1895-1898), I, xix.
9. *Gleanings*, II, 27.
10. Letter to Sophia Lady Bute, 15 July 1850, collection of Lord Bute at Mount Stuart.
11. Letter to Louisa Bromley, 7 February 1836, Bodleian MS. Eng. lett. d. 377, fol. 44.
12. Transcribed in a letter from Mrs Harriet Polwarth to Lady Louisa Stuart, [1831], Bodleian MS. Eng. lett. c.392, fols. 2-4.
13. Typed transcript of letter to Lady Caroline Gardiner, 1 December 1838, Bodleian MS. Eng. lett. c.393, fol. 174.
14. Letter from Sir Walter Scott, 7 February 1826, *The Letters of Sir Walter Scott*, ed. H. J. C. Grierson (London: Constable, 1932-1937), IX, 420.
15. Bodleian MS. Eng. poet. d.202, fols. 23-24.
16. Transcript of letter to Lady Montagu, [1824], Douglas Home papers, S.R.O. ref. TD.80/33, box 106/7, fol. 10.
17. Transcript of letter to Mrs William Alison, 8 June 1839, Douglas Home papers, S.R.O. ref. TD.80/33, box 104/4, fol. 33.
18. Letter to Lady Montagu, 21 June 1817, Douglas Home papers, S.R.O. ref. TD.80/33, box 104/3, fol. 14.
19. Letter to Sir Walter Scott, 27 January 1818, National Library of Scotland MS.3889, fols. 10-11.

20. Letter to Lady Montagu, [1829], Clinton letters, II, 200.
21. Douglas Home papers, S.R.O. ref. TD.80/33, box 191, bundle 1.
22. Thomas Carlyle, "Biography", *Fraser's Magazine*, 5, No. 27 (April 1832), 259.

PUBLISHED WORKS OF LADY LOUISA STUART

Gleanings From an Old Portfolio, Containing Some Correspondence Between Lady Louisa Stuart and Her Sister Caroline, Countess of Portarlington and Other Friends and Relations. Ed. Mrs Godfrey Clark. 3 vols. Edinburgh: David Douglas, 1895–1898.

"Introductory Anecdotes" to *The Letters and Works of Lady Mary Wortley Montagu*. Ed. Lord Wharncliffe. London: Richard Bentley, 1837. Rev. ed. with a Memoir by W. Moy Thomas. 2 vols. London: George Bell, 1887. Also included in Lady Mary Wortley Montagu, *Essays and Poems*. Ed. Robert Halsband and Isobel Grundy. London: Oxford University Press, 1977.

The Letters of Lady Louisa Stuart. Selected with an Introduction by R. Brimley Johnson. London: John Lane; New York: Lincoln MacVeagh, 1926.

Letters of Lady Louisa Stuart to Miss Louisa Clinton. Ed. James A. Home. 2 vols. Edinburgh: David Douglas, 1901–1903.

Notes by Lady Louisa Stuart on "George Selwyn and His Contemporaries" by John Heneage Jesse. Ed. W. S. Lewis. New York: Oxford University Press; London: Humphrey Milford, 1928.

Selections From the Manuscripts of Lady Louisa Stuart. Ed. James Home. New York and London: Harper, 1899. This volume includes "Some Account of John, Duke of Argyll, and His Family".

Lady Louisa Stuart, 1757–1851
Daughter of the 3rd Earl of Bute
Chalk sketch by John Hayter, London 1837
Collection of Mrs Patricia Maxwell-Scott

Lady Frances Scott
Joshua Reynolds
National Gallery of Scotland

Genealogical Table

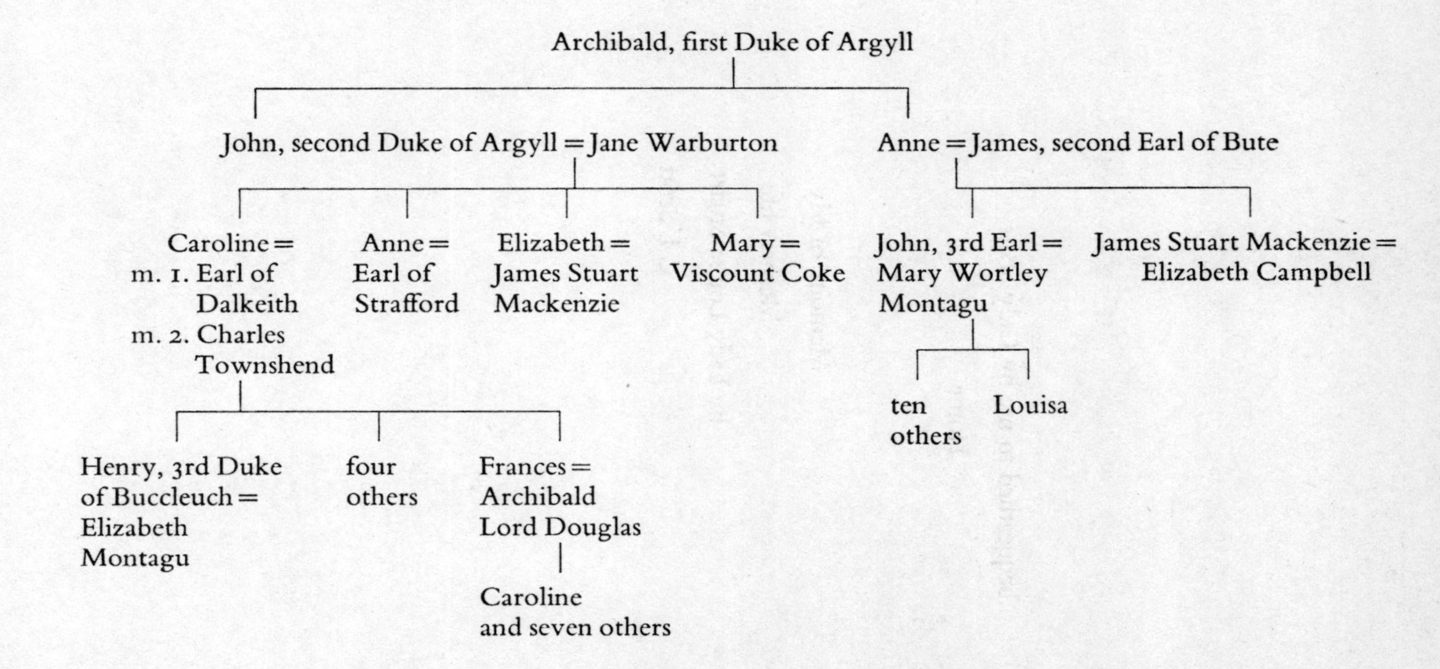

bequeathed to me by Lady Scott

Home

Memoire of My

Mothers life

by Lady Louisa Stuart

C L Scott

You were forewarned, dear Car, that Lady Greenwich's portrait would be reserved for your private perusal. I fear I cannot sketch it with tolerable impartiality. She always does and will present herself to my mind as a wicked witch, a malignant fairy, the Carabosse[1] or Fanfreluche of the tales that amused my childhood. An idea not peculiar to me; for all my contemporaries would have said the same thing. But to this proverb—"the Devil is good-humoured when he is pleased"—we may tack on another, *viz*—the Devil has something pleasant in him (or plausible at least) while he is young. As she had undoubtedly been the object of more than one man's choice, her mind like her person, must once have appeared in a form less repulsive than that it wore in old, or even middle age. And indeed there was a feature of her character, un-amiable in itself, which perhaps enabled her to attract the other sex as long as she could be called—a *fine young* woman—that epithet belonging of right to all dukes' daughters and rich heiresses not positively ugly. She differed from her sisters[2] in having more acuteness and less sincerity. You saw the worst of them, whole and uppermost, unshadowed by disguise or self command; if you chose to search out the good that counterbalanced it, that was your affair: they stirred not a finger to assist you. Now she on the contrary could put on a fair seeming, could make the best of herself where she saw occasion; in coarser terms could *cant*: and what had become canting long ere I knew her, her companions—much more her lovers—might accept as sensibility and sentiment before she turned the corner of thirty. In those early days she had also a grain of romance; of the species which, being factitious, not of native growth—

[1] The evil fairy in *The Sleeping Beauty* who imposes the curse of the poisoned spindle upon the infant Princess Aurora.

[2] The four daughters of John, 2nd Duke of Argyle, were Lady Caroline, Lady Anne, Lady Elizabeth, and Lady Mary Campbell. See Table p. 27.

"—Plays round the head, but comes not near the heart—"[1] and though a flourishing ornament to conversation, tends ultimately to deaden or extinguish those feelings which it gives us the habit of continually exaggerating.

An anecdote may throw light on the subject. In my father's latest years, my poor mother and I, talking carelessly before him, chanced to speak of Lady Greenwich as ill-tempered. He interrupted us with surprise—"What can you mean?—" She must be strangely altered then—"Lady Mary was ever a termagant but I used to think Lady Dalkeith—Lady Caroline—surely a most gentle creature"—she was *his* relation, so we had got upon slippery ground; and my mother who, I saw, did not care to dispute the point with him, cast down her eyes, suppressing a smile. I held my peace too but involuntarily looked up to stare. However a moment's reflection told me how the matter stood. There are few individuals who have not some phrase of their own, some favourite word, which you must be familiar with them to understand as they use it. By—"a *gentle creature*"—my father's highest praise for any thing female—he meant what in Scotland is termed *a sweet girl*—a sweet woman—a character that always imposed upon him; as in truth it does upon most men. Do not you know the mild subdued accents of this sweet species?—Time might easily have made of them the hypocritical whine Lady G.'s sharp tones could sink into, when lamenting over a worthy man mis-used by his coquette wife, or pitying excellent parents for having a rantipole daughter. She never was so disagreeable as when playing in this benevolent key; it seemed the cat velveting her paws and purring while in act to spring: and accordingly the more tender her concern for poor injured A. the heavier fell her censures on B., C. and D., at whom you could clearly see her taking aim from the beginning.

I remember a passage in Marivaux, as far as it goes, very applicable to Lady Greenwich—"*des gens toujours regardant, toujours écoutant, jamais pensant; je les compare à un homme qui passeroit sa vie*

[1] Pope, *Essay on Man*, Epistle IV, l. 254: "Plays round the head but comes not to the heart."

à se tenir à sa fenêtre"[1]—But this does not describe her *all*, as Horace Walpole found means to do with one lucky expression; he christened her—*The Morning Post*—when that paper was newly set up, published in a new manner by fellows blowing deafening horns about the streets and made the vehicle of a sort of scandal the daily prints had 'till then been free from. Public characters were defamed at all times, facts misrepresented, and current reports given, whether false or true; but Mr and Mrs Such a one, who had no concern with politics, and kept within the bounds of common decorum, remained, as they ought to be, unmolested by the press. The original editor of the Morning Post,[2] a half-gentleman half-adventurer, not admitted into tolerable society but hovering on it's outskirts, near enough to catch glimpses of what was going forward, and pick up chambermaids' tattle, began the practice of filling his columns with the vile and mischievous trash in question. If a young married woman—ever so respectable—danced twice with the same man at Almacks[3] or conversed with him for half an hour at the Opera, the next day you saw it recorded and commented upon in the Morning Post; which sometimes named names outright, sometimes gave initials nobody could mistake, sometimes stabbed yet deeper by mysterious hints, sure to kindle every one's curiosity.

Now for the likeness—Lady Greenwich sallied every morning at the earliest visiting hour, entered the first house she found open, and there, in a voice rivalling the horn, published all the matches intrigues and divorces she had heard of; predicted as many more; descanted on the shameful behaviour of the women and the scandalous profligacy of the men; wondered what the world would come to—then bawled a little on public events, made war or peace; and, having emptied her whole budget, packed it afresh to carry it to another door, and another, and another, until

[1] *La Vie de Marianne*, VII, 62, 5.

[2] Henry Bate, who assumed the name of Dudley in 1780.

[3] The assembly rooms in King's Street, St James's, where balls were held for subscribers. Almacks was managed by a committee of ladies of rank who screened candidates for admission.

dinner-time called her home. The rounds of the newspaper were not a bit more regular or certain.

Knowing you as I do, my dear Car, I can suppose a thought is now stealing upon you which you doubt whether you ought or ought not to indulge: namely, that I am too bitter, that it could not be exactly thus, that satire seldom conveys pure truth, that almost all human beings have some redeeming qualities—But I told you at first it was out of my power to be impartial: I *am* bitter on the subject: I was born so; for the subject and the bitter feeling came to me together, as you will presently find. You must have remarked in many a melancholy instance that where a child is born after it's father's death, or just before it's mother's, it usually becomes the darling of the surviving parent; cherished as more immediately, more sacredly connected with the deceased, than any of it's brothers and sisters. They have suffered the same deprivation, perhaps a greater evil; since some of them may be of an age to feel and deplore their loss; therefore Reason would bid us compassionate them the most; but Nature turns to the poor little helpless unconscious being so sorrowfully ushered into a rough world, half the protection due to it already snatched away. And kind wise Nature seems resolved to double it's hold upon what yet remains. If the widower weeps in agony over his motherless babe, with what sensations must the widow await the birth of an infant doomed never to know a father?

Nevertheless there are exceptions to this general rule, and Lady Greenwich was a most marked one. She grieved immoderately for Lord Dalkeith's untimely death,[1] fell into fits, closed her windows, and kept her room a considerable time. In all which there might be no feigning; She had had in every sense a very great loss: she was unused to govern her passions, and no doubt felt truly sorry for herself. But my charitable constructions will go no farther; nor yet can I rest satisfied with saying this affliction failed to inspire a peculiar affection for Lord Dalkeith's posthumous child. Negatives are insufficient. There could not be more decided, rooted, undisguised aversion—and this as I believe, from first to last. At least, I never heard of a time when better

[1] Francis, Earl of Dalkeith, died 1 April 1750.

feelings prevailed: nor did *She*, whose mild candid spirit would have rejoiced to make the acknowledgement, ever hint that at some remote period she could recollect having been, even transiently, the object of maternal tenderness.

Should you ask how I learned this circumstance, I could no more tell you than I could who taught me to know my right hand from my left. I found it an allowed established point which nobody dreamed of questioning; as quietly taken for granted as it was that other people loved their children. That the two persons existed, and that the mother disliked the daughter, were facts admitted into my mind at once and linked fast together in my remembrance. When quite a child, before I ever saw *F.*, I used to hear the aunts[1] mention her in a commiserating tone—"Ah poor Frances!—Frances, you know, is not a favourite; poor thing!"—And I never inquired why they pitied her, for it seemed as if I had always known.

It is difficult to trace the causes of such unnatural hatreds, which sometimes appear almost as instinctive as a mother's fondness itself. That we speak of might originate from an extraordinary portion of selfish vanity operating, without check or counteraction, upon a heart which, I am persuaded, never felt real affection for any thing human; father, mother, husband, son, or daughter. It is almost absurd to dread paining you by what will follow, yet I pause—We scarcely know whether our parents are handsome or ugly: 'though ever so young, they are old in our eyes, therefore not beautiful; on the other hand, we are too familiar with their outward form to observe it's defects. You may then be ignorant that *F.* was always held remarkable for the reverse of beauty; as much so, for example, as the Norths at a later time. This was the general opinion, fully assented to by her own family, and above all by herself. Her constant joking on the subject made it an easy one to others; yet I remember her once saying seriously and sadly to my sister Caroline—"Though I laugh it off, I can tell you my lot is hard; for nobody admires beauty more than I do, and unluckily *white* ugliness happens to

[1] See note 2, p. 29.

displease my taste more than *black*:[1] I do assure you that when I rise in a morning, it turns me half sick to look at my own face in the glass"—Oh what a weight of mental excellence nature threw into the opposite scale!—But once more for Lady Dalkeith—While she was enjoying the sympathy of her friends and engrossing her own attention in the interesting character of an afflicted widow, the neglected infant was probably left to the care of it's nurse, not thought of at all. When it began to attract notice, the selfish mother viewed it with mortification and ill-will, because it wanted charms to draw down encomiums from her silly visitors. And afterwards, when this mother, no longer very youthful had by her second marriage (which took place when *F.* was five years old) a second brood of children, extolled as pretty, the plain little girl, now beyond the age of a plaything, fell into greater disgrace than ever.

Both good and evil are apt to flow from unthought of sources. Who would have dreaded evil from a mother?—Or foreseen that the instrument of good was to be a step-father, noted for any thing rather than strictness of principle; a dissipated man, who in the prime of life, at just thirty, had married for interest-sake a disagreeable woman six or seven years older than himself?—Not mere sordid interest however; since her connections and the guardianship of her eldest son rendered her a prize tempting to his ambition. And what tempted her?—She would have told you passionate love alone—I say the impulse of a passion, not love in my dictionary, mingled with a superabundance of vanity allured first by his splendid public reputation, and finally captivated by the fame of his success with other women.

He already shone as one of those distinguished men sure to govern or to agitate a country like ours. Such a person (but that his career proved shorter) as the elder or younger Pitt, as Charles Fox, or as Canning; with talents equally great for business and for oratory. After holding various high offices, he died at forty two, chancellor of the exchequer and leader of the House of Commons, having just obtained a peerage for his family, given to Lady Dalkeith and limited to her sons by him. The great seal was

[1] Referring to hair color or shade of complexion.

scarcely put to the patent creating her baroness of Greenwich when a sudden illness hurried him out of this world. As I think you have not Burke's works, where he is pourtrayed with a masterly hand—in the speech on American taxation—I will transcribe the whole passage.

> —After speaking of Lord Chatham—"Even before this splendid orb was entirely set; on the opposite quarter of the horizon arose another luminary, and, for his hour, became lord of the ascendant.
>
> "This light too is passed and set for ever. You understand, to be sure, that I speak of Charles Townshend, officially the re-producer of this fatal scheme; whom I cannot even now remember without some degree of sensibility. In truth, Sir, he was the delight and ornament of this house, and the charm of every private society which he honoured with his presence. Perhaps there never arose in this country, nor in any country, a man of a more perfect and finished wit, and (where his passions were not concerned) of a more refined, exquisite and penetrating judgement. If he had not so great a stock as some have had who flourished formerly, of knowledge long treasured up, he knew better by far than any man I ever was acquainted with how to bring together within a short time, all that was necessary to establish, to illustrate, and to decorate that side of the question he supported. He stated his matter skillfully and powerfully. He particularly excelled in a most luminous explanation and display of his subject. His style of argument was neither trite and vulgar, nor subtle and abstruse. He hit the house just between wind and water—And not being troubled with too anxious a zeal for any matter in question, he was never more tedious nor more earnest than the preconceived opinions, and present temper of his hearers required; to whom he was always in perfect unison. He conformed exactly to the temper of the house; and seemed to lead because he was always sure to follow it. . . .

"... It would be an invidious thing to remark the errors into which the authority of great names has brought the nation, without doing justice at the same time to the great qualities whence that authority arose. The subject is instructive to those who wish to form themselves on whatever of excellence has gone before them. There are many young members in the house (such of late has been the rapid succession of public men) who never saw that prodigy, Charles Townshend, nor of course knew what a ferment he was able to excite in every thing, by the violent ebullition of his mixed virtues and failings. For failings he had undoubtedly—many of us remember them; we are this day considering the effects of them. But he had no failings which were not owing to a noble cause; to an ardent, generous, perhaps an immoderate passion for fame; a passion which is the instinct of all great souls. He worshipped that goddess wheresoever she appeared; but he paid his particular devotions to her in her favourite habitation, her chosen temple, the House of Commons. ...

"... Among vices there is none which the House abhors in so great a degree as *obstinacy*. Obstinacy, Sir, is certainly a great vice, and frequently the cause of great mischiefs. It happens however, very unfortunately, that the whole line of the great and masculine virtues, constancy, gravity, magnanimity, fortitude, fidelity, and firmness, are closely allied to this disagreeable quality, of which you have so just an abhorrence; and in their excess all these virtues may easily fall into it. He who paid such a punctilious attention to all your feelings certainly took care not to shock you by that vice which is the most disgustful to you. ...[1]

You may perceive Burke designs to intimate that this dazzling genius was versatile, unsteady, and too fond of applause. Nor could his best friends have denied these to be the draw backs on

[1] The speech was delivered in the House of Commons on 19 April 1774. Lady Louisa's quotation is likely to be somewhat inexact.

his excellence as a statesman. But you will think his private character more our concern.

This was careless, gay, inconsiderate, volatile, seemingly foreign to every serious reflection or feeling. He had one of those happy tempers which nothing can ruffle, without a grain of pride sternness or resentment in his nature. Ready to laugh with every body and at every thing, he poured out wit in torrents; and it was so much the worse for truth if ever truth stood in wit's way. Most people addicted to romancing are their own heroes, tell marvellous stories of themselves, which he did not do, being no egotist; but when once he had sprung the rattle adieu to strict veracity. Possibly he enjoyed what is now called *mystifying* his hearers and making grave folks stare; for I heard instances of his fertile invention chiefly from Lord Strafford the most matter of fact person on earth, and Mr Mackenzie who was apt to be mysterious and political; while *F.* never appeared aware of his having such a propensity: whence I conclude that he checked it, and was always in earnest with her. Tell what stories of him they would however, I could perceive that these others dwelt on his memory with regret, as if they had delighted in his society.

The first time I was in Scotland, I found people whose recollections were still fresh of what passed when he and lady Dalkeith came down to visit her son's estates soon after their marriage. Business required this; and she had no objection either to show the Natives her admired young husband, or to display her own consequence to him. The second object she attained; for at that time high rank and fortune were so venerated there, that the honours paid her might have done for a duke of Wellington now: but a man of the world like Mr Townshend, and one of his character, was not to be overawed by seeing the Edinburgh baillies cringe to my lady his wife; and their evident contempt for the younger brother she had condescended to take in tow, instead of mortifying or angering him, afforded him great amusement. The City gave her a feast; the lord provost stood ready in white gloves to hand her from her carriage; the assembly —judges, magistrates, literati and all—bowed to the ground at her entrance: while he, altogether unnoticed, followed humbly in her train—but not silently, for he exclaimed aloud—"Nay! God bless you gentlemen! Do remember I am George prince of Denmark at least"—So when some old retainers of the Buccleuch family gained an audience—"Ah! said she in her softest whine—"Observe the attachment of these poor people—Affectionate creatures! They are crying for joy to see me"—"Do'n't be too sure of that, lady Dalkeith. I believe, if the truth were known, it's for sorrow to see *me*"—Many other such anecdotes have probably faded from my memory.

With regard to women he was without doubt a man of pleasure, a libertine: yet still no seducer of innocence, nor one who would take much pains to win those who did not meet him half way; which all the fine ladies of his time were so disposed to do that he had little occasion to wander in quest of shyer game. I am now representing him as the world saw and generally thought of him. You will shortly behold him in another light. After all, it would have been miraculous if he had issued forth a saint from such a school of morality as his mother's house. Let me give you a sketch of the Townshend family.

His grandfather, the second viscount Townshend, for some time George the first's chief minister, left a respectable name in History. His father's was less conspicuous. I never heard any thing of him, good or bad, but that he was the famous lady Townshend's husband—it is to be presumed a peaceable one, since to *famous* you may assuredly prefix another syllable, and judge of her wit, her impudence and profligacy, by her being the known original of those two admirable portraits, Fielding's lady Bellaston,[1] and lady Tempest in Pompey the little.[2] The very incident of lady Bellaston's picking up Tom Jones at the masquerade was supposed to be grounded upon an adventure of Lady Townshend's with one of the lovers of low degree whom she stooped to keep in pay, after the lovers of high had flown off along with the beauty that had once attracted them. Down to

[1] In *Joseph Andrews* (1742).

[2] Francis Coventry, *The History of Pompey the Little*: or, *The Life and Adventures of a Lap-Dog* (1751).

her old age however and my own early time, men of all sorts—aye, the gravest—were fond of her conversation: for you know how they relish indecency and scandal, even without the sauce of wit, much more with a profusion of it. I saw her once or twice, but it was with her granddaughter; and in our company the odious old beldame thought herself bound to talk virtuously and preach, which created disgust. Had she kept to her own proper style, I might have laughed at her jokes without suspecting their meaning.

This renowned lady had an only daughter, whose chance, bad in itself, was the worse for her being very pretty. She lost her character, married obscurely, and ceased to be talked of. For the sons, entering the gay world long before their good mother had done with it, they found her a most indulgent confidante in their love-affairs, and, if necessary, a Madame Commode.[1] Knowing all this—for every body knew it—Lady Dalkeith boldly flung herself and her children into the hands of the second brother; and, as most people agreed in opinion with Lord Orford, whose ironical remarks on the match I once pointed out to you,[2] they were absolutely baulked by the decency of Mr T.'s behaviour, and his making a kind and attentive, 'though perhaps not a very constant, husband. No one could be persuaded that this was any thing but excellent acting, playing the amiable, a copy of his countenance, and so forth. Even my mother, never prone to judge uncharitably, spoke with a sort of doubt about the concern she saw him show, when lady Dalkeith's youngest son, James Scott, died of a fever at ten years old. During the course of the disease, the mother sate receiving visitors, hearing news, and inveighing against her neighbours' sins as at other times: while Mr Townshend was anxiously expecting the physician, hurrying out of the room to question him, sending for more advice, and

[1] i.e., a bawd.

[2] Possibly in Walpole's *Memoires of the Last Ten Years of the Reign of George the Second* (London, 1822). He quotes Townshend: "It was at the same period he said, when the struggle about Lord Bute was depending, 'Silly fellow for silly fellow, I think it is as well to be governed by my uncle with a blue ribband, as by my cousin with a green one.' " (II, 64-65).

going up and down stairs without his shoes for fear of disturbing the patient. In this and other instances I believe he deserved more credit than the world inclined to give him; for he was good-natured and had the sufferer before his eyes. *F.* described him as very fond of his own children; and it could not be surer that he drew breath than that he sincerely, fervently, heartily loved one creature beside—more than them, more than his interest, his pleasure, or any thing else upon earth—This dearest of all objects was no other than *F.* herself—Now you know why I bade you keep his picture—

Granting he did feel himself in some measure piqued to falsify the predictions usual on a rich widow's imprudent marriage, the vulgar cry he knew to be current, that he would soon lock up the foolish woman, and turn her children adrift; yet the very desire of *playing amiable* (as it is called) might insensibly lead him to imbibe true affection. The boys were at school; he caressed the girl as nearest at hand; the girl clung to him in return. He had powers of entertainment for all ages; and think how his gay good humour, his indulgence, his playfulness, must have charmed a poor child un-used to any sort or shape of kindness: 'till then always snubbed, humbled, mortified, and kept in the back ground. Her mother's unnatural antipathy might well add the impulse of compassion to other motives swaying a mind far from ungenerous: and there is one blessed thing in the human heart, a remnant of the divine likeness which survived the fall; I mean the re-action of benevolence, it's tendency to re-produce itself: we cannot serve or benefit any of our fellow-creatures but it invariably begets some portion of regard for them in our own bosoms. Conscious of being the poor little thing's sole protector, and almost engrossing all her affection, his partiality for her naturally increased. As did in proportion Lady Dalkeith's ill-will. She felt his tenderness for the object she disliked a reproach to herself, and an injury to the Townshend babies, who had an exclusive right to all the love he could bestow; not as *his* children, but as his children by *her*.

Small things often make a deep impression on young minds; and justly; for they mark characters more strongly than actions which admit of premeditation. You know how *F.* read aloud—the voice still dwells in our ears. When about eleven years old, she had one day so delighted Mr Townshend with her manner of reading to him, that on Lady Dalkeith's coming into the room he unadvisedly expressed his surprise and admiration. On this, her ladyship flew at him like a tyger, reproaching him in the bitterest terms for his injustice, his caprice, his unnatural preference of that odious frightful girl to his own dear sweet beautiful children (who were not old enough to read at all). Here was a proof of it—nobody could read worse, as he very well knew, whatever he chose to say—"but to be sure every thing *She* does is to be cried up to the skies; and I suppose to please you, one must read quick and thick like Frances!"—*F.* said the effect this had upon her could scarcely be conceived; it was iron entering her soul; she felt crushed beyond the power of ever rising again; attributing all Mr Townshend's praises and encouragement to mere good nature, for he knew how ill she read and did every thing else—she had heard him told so—Several months passed before she could again read aloud even to herself alone: if she attempted it—"*Quick and thick like Frances*"—seemed re-echoed by the walls, and a choking in her throat would not let her go on.

When such storms arose (and they were frequent) Mr T. was not backward to use the advantage man has over woman by taking his hat and marching out of the premises, or burying himself in the depths of his official papers: but he had not the gift which man ought to have, to silence even a scold by the calm resolution that speaks him master. Want of firmness, his chief political defect, operated at his own fire-side; and instead of being, as the malicious had foretold, Lady Dalkeith's tyrant, he was in reality afraid of her. This might diminish his power of protecting her daughter (openly at least) but in process of time it created an additional tie between the daughter and him: they were fellow-sufferers, who sought peace and consolation in each other's society. Thus thrown together, Burke tells you what She had to see in the most brilliant man of the age; and that man's quick penetration very, *very* early discerned the wit, the taste, the soundness of head, the perfect sweetness of temper, the thousand excellencies to be found in her. He strove to cultivate her mind, directed her reading, read with her, reasoned with her and ever treated her as a rational being. In short, by the time she was fifteen, from his favourite plaything she had grown into his confidential friend, to whom he freely unbosomed himself, and with whom he discussed all manner of subjects, not excepting those which concerned the state. I have heard her say she could scarcely believe her own memory on looking back to days when she felt the warmest interest in parliamentary proceedings, longed to learn the numbers of a division, and was all anxiety for his return home that she might hear what had passed between him and Mr Pitt (Lord Chatham) or some other statesman. When also, if accidentally present at the visits such persons paid him, she did not lose a word of the conversation, nor scruple afterwards to give her opinion of it: which he would combat or rectify if he thought it erroneous, but never set aside with—"Child, what should you know of the matter?—"

Here we may perceive the origin of that dislike to talk politics and indifference about them so remarkable in her ever since you—nay ever since *I*—knew her. She had tasted them at the fountain-head; there was no going higher than Charles Townshend: therefore she could never be actuated by the vanity that sets most female politicians in motion. She had likewise seen affairs of importance so near as to know the mischief and folly of women's meddling with them; to have observed how rarely the men principally concerned (on whichsoever side) make them the subject of their common conversation; and consequently to be aware what a risk of talking nonsense is incurred, by those flies on the chariot wheel who would fain buzz about nothing else. Add, that after Mr T. vanished from the scene, she lived in constant intimacy with people directly opposed to each other in party: the husband of her dearest friend being nearly at the head of one faction,[1] her brother and all her family adhering to the other: so she daily heard the arguments and regretted the violence of both.

[1] The 3rd Duke of Portland, Whig politician, who served as Prime Minister April–December 1783, as Home Secretary 1794-1801, and again as Prime Minister 1807-1809.

Frances, Lady Douglas
2nd wife of 1st Lord Douglas, 1750–1817
Miniature by F. Ferriere about 1794
Collection of Earl of Home

Caroline Lucy Douglas

Self-portrait (1807) as Constance discovering the armour of de Wilton in Marmion

In a private Scottish collection

A position which could hardly fail to render a person of her clear understanding moderate, if not neutral.

To resume her early history—She described herself as having been full of contradictions; the exuberance of her spirits making her the greatest romp imaginable when out of Lady D.'s chilling presence. So that while this moment she was considering Mr T.'s plans for the government of the nation, the next saw her engaging with all her heart in any youthful or childish amusement. Education (in the modern sense) she had none: there was not much for any body in those days, and Lady Dalkeith grudged the expence of the most ordinary masters, especially of such as improve the carriage and manner. *F.* never was taught to dance—"of what use could it be to a girl whom one would wish nobody to look at?"—When grown up, being fond of dancing, she found this a perpetual mortification—"If asked, I cannot resist it (said she) and yet I know I make myself ridiculous. I see the bystanders turn aside to laugh, and then go and ask who it is that trundles about so comically—" I almost think you must have heard her describe what her distress was when she found herself placed at the head of a set, with the foolish duke of Cumberland for her partner, to begin a ball which Lady G. gave a little before her son's marriage.

You cannot doubt that her dress was equally economical, and bare clothing thought sufficient for a figure which Lady Greenwich rejoiced to believe no ornaments could render tolerable. On the other hand, Mr Townshend did not concern himself about ladies' accomplishments, nor see any want of them in the delightful companion of his leisure hours, who reasoned more justly than most of the men he knew, had more power to entertain him, and more taste for his favourite authors. How she was dressed, whether she was pretty or ugly, and danced well or ill, or not at all, escaped his observation. If she had applied to him for masters, he would have given her the best and dearest in London, and left Lady Dalkeith to fret over the cost while he repaired to the House of Commons or the Council-board. But besides that *F.* must have staid at home to bide the brunt of the tempest, she had from the very beginning a delicacy an instinctive sense of right, a dignity of mind, which would not let her avail herself of his indulgence to gain any point directly contrary to Lady Dalkeith's will.

The same nicety of feeling produced an invincible repugnance ever to ask him for pocket-money. Lady Dalkeith by no chance gave her any, and he sometimes did not think of it for a good while together. Whenever he did, it came showering upon her, even in her very childhood, with far greater profusion than was good for her: whence resulted habits of carelessness and extravagance which she confessed she had cause subsequently to lament having contracted. In truth, if one deliberately purposed to give a young person such habits, one could devise no fitter means than distressing privation at one time, superabundance at another, and uncertainty reigning always.

When *F.* and my two sisters, Augusta and Caroline, advanced towards womanhood, the cousins were to be acquainted; which led to my seeing her for the first time. She came one evening before seven o'clock—the hour of tea when people dined at four. I was about nine years old, and as if I had had a presentiment what she was to be to me, it made so strong an impression that I can now shut my eyes and call up the whole scene—where she sate, how she looked, how she spoke—every minute particular. Ages were then marked by dress; she wore a grown woman's, and was in deep mourning, either for her brother Campbell, or the Duchess of Argyll.[1] I remember she flirted a black crape fan in my face, saying something that set me a laughing. I thought I had never seen so agreeable a person, and longed to have her come again: but I do not recollect that she did, nor that I saw her any more 'till I too was an *adolescente*, and the same reasons of cousinhood threw *Miss Townshend* and me together.

I believe my sisters did not much suit *F.* nor she them, for they were as yet mere girls, of unformed minds, and would have understood a common-place character better. Her friendship with Caroline commenced some years later, after poor Augusta married. However a moderate intercourse subsisted, and they occasionally went to drink tea with her in her own room; where (by what I overheard them say) Lady Dalkeith never appeared;

[1] Campbell Scott died 18 October 1766 at the age of 18. The Duchess of Argyll, Lady Frances' grandmother, died 16 April 1767.

but Mr Townshend would often join the party and converse with the utmost ease and good humour.

I shall not wonder if you infer from all I tell you, that *F.* could scarcely lead a very wretched life, blessed with such a friend—or father—Yet after all, she was under Lady Dalkeith's authority; and many are the ways in which women can teize and torment women, unperceived by a male spectator; who may hinder open violence, ward off a dagger offered at the breast, but can do nothing to prevent thorns from vexing the thing that is raw, and pins from pricking a sensitive part to the quick. Daily and hourly sneers, taunts, scolding and fault finding, had pretty much these effects; and unless Mr Townshend fought a battle which for more reasons than one she dreaded to see him engaged in, she was regularly denied every little gratification there could be a decent pretext to with-hold. Nor did her keen sensibility of heart, joined to nerves constitutionally weak, ever admit of her growing callous; so that Lady Dalkeith enjoyed the vengeful pleasure of plaguing her to her full content. Vengeful, I say; since, as you may guess, her ladyship beheld Mr Townshend's fondness for her with bitter resentment. Not that she really liked his company or would ever have given up half an hour's gossipping to sit with him in his study; but the dog in the manger has abundance of likenesses upon two legs; and she could not brook that *F.* should be the person to fill the place she had wilfully deserted; or rather the place she had never sought to occupy. If indeed he had noticed the girl only as a girl, made her fetch and carry, and disregarded her silly prattle, it might have been borne with patience: the sting lay in the confidence he reposed in her, and the high opinion of her understanding he did not strive to conceal.

But we are not come to the severe part of *F*'s trial. I learned much more on the subject than I had ever before known or suspected during my long stay at Bothwell in the year 1800; when, I own to you, I sometimes ventured to remonstrate against an ignorance of worldly matters which I thought too profound in—"*The Happy Valley*"—Oh! How happy to us all!—Having chanced to see ill effects in two or three instances from what I will call a *childish* education, (an incorrect term, but you know my meaning) I was adverse to it, and argued accordingly.—"Consider, (said I) what a very different person were you at the same age—" *F.* always stopped my mouth with an answer that precluded any reply—"Ah! No matter for that—If you did but know how deeply unhappy I was at the time you speak of, what agitation and misery I suffered, you would think it natural I should wish to prolong for THEM the period of innocent enjoyment, and delay the moment of acquaintance with the world."

Such discourse led her by degrees to say more; and I almost started on finding that Mr Townshend's partiality had itself given her unspeakable pain, by exciting continual uneasiness at it's excess, and terrifying apprehensions of it's nature. Do not mistake me however—he never was guilty of the least impropriety, never made the most distant approach to any personal freedom. He idolized her mind alone; seeming hardly to recollect she had a person: and perhaps the very consciousness that there was nothing sensual in his passion rendered him the less solicitous to put any curb upon it. But still *passion* it was—passion marked by it's engrossing tendency, it's overwhelming and uncontrollable force: in which she could not help feeling a something distinct from the paternal tenderness he used to show her. She acknowledged in short, that although no such idea presented itself to her at the time, yet on recalling and considering all that passed she could have little doubt that the unhappy man to whom she owed so much and who was so dear to her, had a tincture of the aweful malady which afterwards broke out openly in some of his descendants.* So truly says the poet—

"Great wit to madness sure is near allied
"And thin partitions do their bounds divide—[1]

From taking pleasure in her company, he at length grew unwilling ever to have her out of his sight; and when they were unavoidably separated (I do not mean for days, but hours) the

*—In his son William Townshend and his grandson Henry Wilson—and (taking another form) in Caroline Wilson's deficiency of understanding.

[1] John Dryden, *Absalom and Achitophel*, ll. 163-164: "Great Wits are sure to Madness near ally'd;/And thin Partitions do their Bounds divide."

most important avocations would not deter him from pouring out his soul to her on paper with all that powerful vehement eloquence which bewitched and bore away his hearers in the senate. No day elapsed without her receiving some letter or note —often sent *open*, and by the footman—the contents of which, the enthusiastic praises and ardent professions of attachment, might have given birth to very injurious surmises if it had fallen into indifferent hands; if into those of her malignant enemy, Lady Dalkeith, would have ruined her for life. As she told me this— "I know," said she—"I am laughed at for my unwillingness to credit stories to the prejudice of others: people ascribe it to simplicity and ignorance of the world; but how can I forget the time when I every day of my life ran the risk of having my character blasted beyond redemption; with the strongest appearances to justify a horrible imputation against me, and no possibility of proving my innocence?—Do you wonder that a voice from within should ask me—may it not be thus also in such or such a case generally held to admit neither of doubt nor palliation?"—

A most cruel part of her situation was that she might say with Juliet

—"My dismal scene I needs must act alone"—[1]

In many kinds of evil it does one good merely to vent oneself, be kindly listened to and pitied: but to whom could she reveal so extraordinary a distress?—Assuredly not to any *young* friend.— And where had she an elder one fitted for the purpose? —Ere you read these pages, you will have seen what her Campbell aunts were, and may judge whether they could answer it. Nor would her father's sister have been more competent to guide and counsel her, though perhaps more likely to hold her tongue.[2] Thrown wholly on the resources of her own mind, her admirable sense and firm principles were her sole support, while under the necessity of daily chiding, soothing, restraining and arguing with that beloved instructor and protector hitherto looked up to as a parent—and her only one. Still we cannot estimate all her

[1] *Romeo and Juliet*, IV, iii, 19.

[2] Lady Jane Scott.

sufferings, nor perceive how the silence and secrecy indispensably requisite tended to aggravate them, unless we take into our account the uncommon openness of a temper not only incapable of deceit but abhorring every species of subterfuge disguise and concealment as some persons loathe particular animals or articles of food. The unnatural position in which it placed her to be always dreading what people might discover what they might think, was far more insupportable to her spirit than it would have been to any other, and compleatly embittered every hour of her existence.

At length a ray of bright sunshine broke through the darkness. The duke returned from his travels, and married within as short a time afterwards as sufficed to mix a little with the world, make acquaintance with Lady Betty Montagu, propose to her, and be accepted.[1] Love—*your* sort of love—I fancy nobody thought of; but there was good liking and preference on both sides; and Lady Betty had a choice; for Lady Macartney has often told me that our eldest brother, then accounted the handsomest man in England, would fain have paid his addresses to her, and met with so chilling a reception at the first advance that he saw it was vain to go a step farther.[2] The effects of this marriage to *F.* will be best told in her own emphatic words, which—uttered as they were with energy—I have often of late years bid myself recall when the poor Duchess's ways have been more than commonly irritating and untoward.—"When I reflect upon it, I protest it looks as if Providence had sent her into the family on purpose to be my guardian angel—" The instant the match was settled, the future bride, and indeed her father and mother, opened their arms wide to embrace *F.*; took her as a sister, a daughter, one of themselves. And lady Dalkeith, whose cue it was to pay them all possible court, found herself reduced to return them awkward unwilling thanks, for kindnesses she would much rather they had let alone.

[1] Elizabeth, daughter of George, Duke of Montagu, married Henry, 3rd Duke of Buccleuch, 2 May 1767.

[2] Jane, second daughter of John, 3rd Earl of Bute, married George, Earl Macartney, 1 February 1768. John, 1st Marquess of Bute, married Charlotte Jane Hickman 12 November 1766.

The first fruit of this connection, a pressing invitation to accompany the new-married couple to Scotland, was to *F.* what a fair prospect of escaping from jail would have been to a prisoner in expectation of the death-warrant. Little did they dream that along with an agreeable jaunt they tendered safety and refuge. But how to avail herself of the offer was another question. Through Mr Townshend's interference only could she hope to obtain a permission which, she knew, sheer ill-nature would determine Lady Dalkeith to refuse: and what chance was there of his willingly consenting to part with her?—She resolved the matter long and broached it fearfully at last; while he listened with deep dejection to all she had to say, but without anger or surprise; taking it as a blow he had made up his mind to expect and submit to. After a mournful pause, he told her he acknowledged it natural that for a thousand reasons she should long to go where novelty and pleasure awaited her; but (alas!) had she not a latent motive still stronger than her desire for these—A secret wish to fly from him?—He dared not blame her for it; though it stung him to the soul—and surely wronged him; for what could she fear from one to whom she was dearer than the life which she alone rendered supportable?—When fatigued with business and harassed by faction, where was he to look for relaxation amusement or sympathy?—What a home had he to return to, uncheered by her!—The trifling annoyances he gave her might perhaps be at an end sooner than she imagined—Well! No matter—She should have a thorough proof how much he preferred her happiness to his own: he would go every length, strain every nerve, to make Lady Dalkeith comply with her desire—So saying, the minister, the orator, the celebrated wit, the man commonly reputed void of feeling, gave way to a passionate burst of it: he covered his face with his hands, and for some minutes cried like a child.

I hardly need add that she told me this scene tore her to pieces: but, conscious it more than ever behoved her to be firm, she did not let it shake her purpose. He, on his part, never uttered another syllable to oppose or lament it, but, faithfully keeping his word, took for once a husband's authority with his perverse wife, to whom he declared in a peremptory tone that the duke had a right to ask for his sister's company; therefore must and should be gratified.

Cannot you picture to yourself the delight of this first distant journey? —All grievances left behind—new objects, new society, and entirely new situation—The duke's known intention of becoming a Scotchman and residing much at a place which had been deserted for almost a century,[1] rendered him and his family beyond measure popular in the neighbourhood; indeed dear to the whole kingdom: while the cordial union already established between *F.* and the dutchess secured to the one her full share of the respect, court, and homage paid the other. Her natural vivacity kindled and had fair play. People themselves endowed with wit and ability found them out in her, were eager to enjoy her conversation, and learned to value her character. Considering too that with a native genuine taste for all that was picturesque, romantic, or poetical, she had 'till now seen only Sudbrook[2] and a very tame dull part of Oxfordshire, the beauties of nature, the view of what Mrs Montagu called "a high-featured country," the variety of rock, mountain torrent, waterfall, and sea-prospect, might fairly excite sensations approaching to rapture.

Thus happily did the summer glide away; but autumn was scarcely begun when an astounding blow recalled every painful thought in the most painful manner. The foreboding Mr Townshend had darkly hinted proved too just. He was seized with a violent illness proceeding from obstruction and inflammation of the bowels; and his physician, Sir Wm. Duncan, though eminent, so grossly mistook his case as to pronounce the danger over, when all pain suddenly ceased and he sunk into apparent slumber; where-as, a mortification having taken place, that slumber was the sure forerunner of death; and accordingly he awaked no more.

The letters announcing this event brought *F.* assurances from her aunts that it had not at all injured the health of Lady Green-

[1] Dalkeith House.

[2] Near Kingston-on-Thames, seat of the dowager Duchess of Argyll, Lady Frances' grandmother.

wich (as we must now style her) that—thank God! she bore it with wondrous fortitude and resignation; and so the extreme anxiety which doubtless *F.* felt on her poor dear mother's account might change to pious gratitude for her being thus supported under her heavy affliction. A vulgar phrase the men are fond of would not be ill applied here. But I believe *F.*, for the only time in her life, had the wisdom to consider herself first, and form a pretty just estimate of what Lady Greenwich was likely *not* to feel on the occasion. Her ladyship's passion (of whatever sort) for Mr Townshend had long been extinguished, therefore being—in plain English—heartily glad to get rid of him, she wore weeds, took the air in a black coach, and assembled gossips and news-mongers at home instead of sallying out to seek them; but, after the first "little month", hardly affected to put on a graver face than usual. *F.* knew this would be the case, and the piercing sorrow preying on her own bosom, had but one alleviation; that she was too far off to see it, and escaped the unfeeling taunts which that very sorrow would perhaps have drawn upon her. Where she was, she had no constraint. The duke and dutchess knew (generally) how kind Mr T. had been to her, and how un-kind Lady Greenwich, and they knew no more: they could not divine the agitating recollections, the melancholy circum-stances envenoming the wound; but thinking it perfectly natural she should grieve as for a father, took all the pains in their power to sooth and console her. Meanwhile her reason could not but whisper her a stinging truth—one which happily no other voice could torture her by suggesting—that it was fortunate for her (and perhaps for himself) he should be thus prematurely removed; since what might—or might not—his wild ungoverned sentiments have led to?—But who that is capable of affection, can fail to understand the wringing pain of being forced to say to oneself on the loss of it's object—"it is best for me—I ought to be thank-ful"—?

I asked *F.* whether she thought Lady Greenwich had ever had any suspicion of the conflicts in Mr Townshend's mind?—She answered, not the smallest. In fact, this personage like Marivaux' man at the window, constantly busy in discussing other people's affairs, knew mighty little of her own, and had no leisure to dive deeply into the souls of those connected with her. The newest piece of scandal carried off her whole attention from what was passing nearer home. Yet *F.* mentioned an extraordinary circumstance, which she said she could not account for. Mr Townshend wanted to give her a diamond ring of very great value that he usually wore on his little finger. She steadily refused accepting it unknown to Lady Greenwich. He offered it again and again. "Well then"—said he one day, after pressing it upon her with particular earnestness—"*I* shall continue to wear it, but remember it is *yours*—your property from this moment"—He died; and you may conclude she durst neither claim the ring nor enquire what became of it. She saw it no more 'till she found it after lady Greenwich's decease, wrapped up in an old piece of paper, indorsed in her hand-writing, grown yellow by time—"*For Frances*"—This looked as if something had passed between her and Mr Townshend on the subject, although she could not find in her heart to let *F.* enjoy the token of his regard while she was able to keep it from her.

I should have noted sooner that Lady Greenwich previous to her second marriage settled her first husband's legacy of £10,000 on his younger children.[1] His successor briefly left her *everything*—so what that was nobody could know, as there were no stamp-duties on probates of wills in those days. The world presumed him to have profited largely by the public money which had passed through his hands; and besides gave him the credit—or discredit—of having embezzled the savings of the Duke of Buccleuch's long minority: for few were forthcoming, and the duke, when of age, found his affairs in terrible confusion. He signed lady Greenwich's accounts however without examination, and only said to Mr Mackenzie and lady Betty—"Respect for my mother will always prevent my complaining of Mr Townshend; but to be sure he was an unlucky guardian for me."

Notwithstanding all this I confidently believe him (Mr T.) to have been guilty of nothing but a careless negligence that injured the minor's affairs along with his own. None can reckon how

[1] Of whom only Lady Frances lived to adulthood.

much waste and mischief may be produced in a course of years by mere *slatterning*—to use our womanish word—and many are the instances of men who manage the public business admirably while their own goes to rack and ruin. But my main reason for exculpating him is, that the money—if *there*—could not have melted away. He did not gamble or keep race-horses; he was not remarkably expensive; Lady Greenwich (with a great income) far otherwise. Now what she left behind her *you*, who shared it, ought to know better than I. Allow for the £10,000 she bequeathed to Mrs Wilson, deduct from your joint portions £30,000, which (first and last) belonged to *F.* herself, and did any immense sum devolve from your grandmother? A part of what did, consisted, I fear, of the arrears of her jointure; which the poor Duke, who somehow floundered on in money difficulties all his life, had been very remiss in paying.

His delicacy and kindness probably secured *F.* from ever hearing him cast a reflection on Mr Townshend's memory, but the aunts, I dare swear, were nothing slack in conveying to her ears all that was most disagreeable: since they constantly (to choose) entertained you with the dis-praises of those they supposed you to love best; and if you writhed under the pain it gave you, so much the better. Without meaning to copy them I own I once told her how much he was blamed for having brought her acquainted with a woman of so doubtful a character, and so strongly suspected of intriguing with himself, as the Dutchess of Grafton.* She denied the first fact assuring me Lady Jane Scott, and not he, had promoted the acquaintance: and the scandal she disbelieved, because at the time he was engaged in flirting with another lady, whom he never introduced to her; but who, being very clever and very cunning, got entrance through a different door—the last you would have expected her to find open. She so wheedled the mistress of the house (who was jealous enough, but rarely in the right place) as to become her first favourite; and F. vowed that the death of this person was the only occasion on which she had ever in her life seen Lady Greenwich appear to feel real sorrow.

* Who was afterwards divorced and became the *Lady Ossory* you remember.

The more closely all the painful thoughts connected with Mr Townshend were locked in *F.*'s own heart, the deeper impression they made. A few years after he died she took an opportunity when travelling alone to go to Adderbury,[1] and stay there some days: she protested the walls seemed to bear the record of the conversations which had passed within them: the old sounds rung in her ears, she almost fancied she saw and was talking to him, and worked herself up to such a pitch of agitation that it was lucky a belief in apparitions did not fasten itself permanently on her mind; for at the moment she could scarcely distinguish between the images memory brought back and those created by fancy.

If I understood her right, I was the first person to whom, at the distance of thirty three years, she intrusted these particulars, and I believe I continued to be the only one who knew them as long as she lived. Am I doing well in revealing them to you? An anxious doubt on this very subject has long delayed my fulfilling my promise. I have pondered it again and again without being able to satisfy my own conscience—Yet God knows that acquits me of betraying her secrets through rashness or levity. But I want you to know fully the singular superiority of her character, to see clearly what she was and all she was; and how can I manifest this, unless I show you the trials she went through, the difficulties she had to struggle with, the nice predicament in which she was placed—at an age when others, still within the pale of childhood, have never been called upon to act, or think, or feel at all?

For now, dearest Car, I must fix your attention on a point which, I could wager thousands, you have hitherto overlooked and which will probably bewilder you (it is not enough to say astonish) when you come to consider it—She was barely SEVENTEEN at the time of Mr Townshend's death—How much of life had she lived ere then!—How much had she seen, heard, known, observed, experienced!—How had every faculty of her mind and feeling of her heart been forced into play! What demands upon her had there not been for prudence, firmness, watchfulness, self-

[1] The Duchess of Argyll's house in Oxfordshire, which Charles Townshend used as his country residence.

command, decision, and all the qualities we look for only in persons of riper years!—

Reflect on this, and you will know what to think of a notion I have seen prevalent that her principal merit was *Simplicity*. In one sense I grant it to have been the great charm of her character, but we undervalue that very simplicity without which we take into our account the wisdom—I do not use too strong a word,—aye, the wisdom, interwoven with it—("Be ye wise as serpents and harmless as doves"—).[1] This people did not always do. I used to be irritated at hearing it sometimes said, if not in a tone of contempt, certainly in one of *superiority*—"Poor dear *F.*! In the simplicity of her heart *she* thinks so and so"—those who uttered it visibly unconscious that *F.* had far more knowledge of the world than themselves, and a sounder, because more cool and unbiased, judgement. *Mais*—"*on ne vaut que ce qu'on se fait valoir*"—[2] *F.*'s total absence of self-conceit, her modest estimate of her own capacity, her proneness to rate others higher than herself, her candour, her moderation, the quiet gentle manner in which she rather proposed than pronounced her opinion, made the assured, the positive, and the dictatorial very coolly take her at her word and set her down as their inferior.

To speak truth something like this might be partly the case with one whom we all respect and she almost worshipped. One who before age and peevishness clouded her mind had as clear and sound a head as I ever met with, but who still was not *her* equal. You are aware I mean the dutchess.[3] Seven years' advantage in age, and that of being the person affording a protection urgently needed, placed her originally upon an eminence to which *F.* looked up, and she never lost the habit afterwards, nor liked to allow the possibility of the other's being mistaken. Yet if by any rare chance they did differ *F.* was sure to be in the right. Nobody saw things more distinctly or decided more wisely than the dutchess, provided both sides of a question lay before her; but where only one presented itself, she would

[1] Matthew 10:16.

[2] Possibly a proverbial version of Rabelais, "Autant vault l'homme comme il s'estime," *Pantagruel*, II, 29.

[3] Elizabeth, Duchess of Buccleuch.

sometimes pronounce too prompt a verdict: and, once pronounced, it was irrevocable. While *F.*, recollecting at first setting out that most questions have two sides, never hasty, never wedded to her own opinion, listened, reflected, turned the subject every way, and understood it well before she formed a conclusion. Her wits had been sharpened by the necessity of acting for herself; her views enlarged both by books and the conversation of Charles Townshend and his friends: the dutchess's naturally excellent understanding a very little warped by prejudices, imbibed from a silly father, a capricious 'though clever mother, and a brother, clever too, but remarkably addicted to what we now stile *Quizzing*[1]—the best fosterer of prejudice I know. That wholesome bitter contradiction, *F.*'s daily diet, had never been put to her grace's lips, either before marriage or after it.

Another thing contributed to make the one accept as no more than her lawful due the deference chearfully paid her by the other. She had a strong clear understanding and a feeling heart, but hardly a conception of enthusiasm, no leaning towards the romantic, nothing approaching to *wit*, *genius*, or imagination: endowments which those born without them are apt to view as incompatible with soundness of intellect; or at best as the fruit and ices and sugar-plums of a desert, opposed to the succulent food that sustains life and satisfies hunger. It was the honest sincere belief of Lady Greenwich and her sisters that *F.* had some quickness in useless trifles, but no common sense. This the dutchess by no means adopted; for she was not dull, and, loving *F.*, she admired her talents as part of her: yet feeling herself quite free from the dominion of fancy, proof against the ignis fatuus which she often saw leading more showy people astray, she undoubtedly deemed her own head the more solid of the two. Where-as it was *F.*'s distinguishing peculiarity to unite every brilliant gift with the firmest principles, the clearest discernment, the coolest judgement. I at least never knew a woman her superior in understanding. That of my dear mother,[2] which even the dutchess bowed to, might perhaps rank first, but it stood upon the same step, not a higher.

[1] Teasing or ridiculing.

[2] Mary, Countess of Bute.

With superficial observers, especially those who, dull and slow themselves, know no ground of attachment but habit, *F.* passed for being apt to take sudden and violent fancies which they were glad to deride as *engoumens*. Never was that French Word so mis-applied. The essence of an *engoument*, it's distinctive mark, is fickleness and caprice: its reign is sure to be brief, and it's object to fall speedily into utter oblivion if not disgrace. *F.* like all people who unite very strong feelings with a very lively imagination, was indeed subject to be suddenly captivated by the appearance of qualities that, striking on those two points of her character, offered her something to love and admire. But in no instance did she grow tired of the shining toy, and fling it slightingly aside for a newer. Often her sudden liking became the basis of firm, fond, inviolable friendship: always of lasting good-will and kindness. Even where the first fair seeming had proved deceitful, where the individual weighed in the balance had been found wanting, her partiality would linger after her esteem was perforce withdrawn. In a word, if she had any characteristic, it was the steadiness of her attachments.

You may remember we often laughingly accused her to her face of loving flattery, and being easily duped by the professions of such people as Betsey Robertson, etc: and she would answer that possibly she did like demonstrations of regard and approbation too well; if they were flattering she could not help it: she would rather be cheated than think all her fellow-creatures insincere. In the mortifications of her youth you may find the root of this propensity. No one was ever so free from the least atom of pride or vanity; but such an aching scar had been left by the scorn and dislike early encountered, that praise always came to her with healing on it's wings, in the benign shape of encouragement; and she felt grateful for it because she was humble, not because she was vain. The dutchess, who is properly speaking neither, spurned fulsome commendations (or any commendations directly offered) with disgust; but the flattery of flatteries, constant assent, went down very smoothly: for she did not suspect that you could agree in opinion with her from any other cause than your own reason and the force of truth.

The same habit, inveterate in *F.*, of undervaluing herself, sometimes led her into a singular mistake respecting the abilities of those she met by chance and knew but slightly. What they said in sober sadness would light on her fancy like a spark of fire on gunpowder, awaken a train of lively images, and produce infinite amusement. Then she never failed to give *them* the whole credit of it: while they perhaps were most quiet dull heavy mortals, entirely guiltless of having harboured the spirit they had unwittingly raised. How often used she to tell us there was something clever or whimsical or entertaining in such or such a one, whom we found very common-place persons; and whom even she was compelled to think so upon farther acquaintance; when she had at last winnowed out her own ideas from theirs.

There is one more point, somewhat allied to the chapter of simplicity, that deserves your attention. We see the bustle made now-a-days about preserving young people's innocence by keeping them ignorant of the existence of evil.—"My girls"—said our friend Lady Charlotte Bury[1]—"never heard of adultery in their lives"—So opposite was *F.*'s training that she heard of little else. As she observed to me herself, nothing is half so *instructive* in certain nameless matters as the gossip of scandal loving old ladies; and she vowed she had gained more insight into the mysteries of iniquity by listening to Lady Greenwich's band of immaculate dowagers, than she could have acquired in the society of people guilty of practicing the vices which it was *their* virtuous delight and the business of their lives to detect and censure. You will may be say this might reasonably tend to sicken rather than corrupt a well-disposed young mind; and it did certainly so operate on her's, giving her an antipathy to scandal that proof itself (as we can remember) could hardly overcome. But look to another quarter—She lived with the man of all men most overflowing with wit and humour; it is true he avoided indelicacy in her presence and carefully forbore jesting on religion; for which she affirmed he had a much greater respect than the world imagined. Yet still his jokes would occasionally take a turn not

[1] Novelist, author of *A Marriage in High Life* (1828) and other works. She was daughter of the 5th Duke of Argyll and wife of Rev. Edward Bury.

strictly correct; and then it was as easy to forbear breathing as to resist laughing. Add to which that young persons of great native quickness, who instantly catch a meaning or perceive an allusion in one case, cannot help doing it more readily than the dull, in another. In spite of all this, never did I in my life, and never will you in yours, meet with such real genuine modesty, such delicacy, such purity of thought and word. It seemed as if her mind had had a moral quality resembling that physical one ascribed (fabulously, I believe) to the ermine. Let the little animal be covered with filth or plunged into a pit of mire, it issues forth with it's white garment spotless and unsullied.

I have taken the opportunity thus to digress and dilate upon particular features of her character here, because the Duke's marriage and Mr Townshend's death made a marked change in her situation; a kind of epoch in a life which (strange to say) had already been long from being eventful. I did not know her personally nor hear much of her 'till five or six years afterwards when her intimacy with poor Caroline increased and mine with Miss Townshend began. In the interim it had become a settled thing that she should go to Scotland every year with the duke and dutchess: their house was her daily resort in town; and money-matters were made easy, for at twenty one she came into possession of six hundred* a year, therefore paid her servants' wages and her chair-hire and commenced an independant existence. You would wonder to hear *how* independant. At three and twenty she was more her own mistress in all points really material, than other unmarried women at almost any age while living under the parental roof; and the world consequently viewed her as already what she jokingly professed to be, a decided old maid privileged to do what she pleased. She paid Lady Greenwich unremitting respect and attention, and from principles of duty would have devoted her time to her if permitted: but Lady G. neither relished nor demanded her company, and provided she had her within the reach of her claws—I mean the power of her ill temper—was content she should go her own way; no more disturbed by any maternal advice, guidance, or direction that

* four per cent interest for her fortune—£15,000.

could be of service to her than if one parent had followed the other to the grave the day she was born. Suppose, for example, that she had fallen into the custom of inviting young men to sup in her dressing-room, Lady Greenwich would have published it to the town and gone about railing at her imprudence just as she would have railed at mine in the same case, but never troubled herself to argue against it with a mother's solicitude.

Do you remark how seldom I call Lady Greenwich *her mother*?—It is not that I intentionally avoid it, but the expression is not natural to me, nor was it so to any-one who knew them. When a stranger used it, *F.*'s friends, taken unawares, felt an odd sort of surprise. Whether she herself in her infancy said Mamà like other children, I cannot tell, but I am very certain the sweet and soothing name, "*my mother*", never at any time fell from her lips in my hearing. As little did "my daughter", or "my dear", from Lady Greenwich's. "*Fra-ances*", pronounced in a particularly disagreeable tone, was the only appellation she ever gave her: and her letters, when kindest, were subscribed "Yours affectionately"—Sometimes barely—"Yours, Greenwich".

There was one curious result from Lady Greenwich's virtual resignation of her proper office; the aunts took upon them to work double tides and claim twice the authority aunts are usually held entitled to. I except Lady Strafford, who never wished or tried to govern any body, and contented herself with doing *F.* all the good offices in her power. But the two others chose to consider her as under their especial tutelage. Both were eminent righters of wrongs, fond of interfering in cases of domestic oppression, and apt to let their indignation against a husband's or a parent's tyranny flame out in a manner which the party aggrieved often had as little reason to thank them for, as the farmer's boy to bless Don Quixote's interposition between him and his master.[1] *F.* was thus protected by them when a child; that is, boldly noticed and caressed in the way that could most gall Lady Greenwich; and, as they estimated this benefit highly themselves they exacted in return nothing less than the implicit obedience of the grown-up woman: or rather, they never allowed her to grow

[1] Part I, chapter 4.

up while they lived. She used to say that all the faults her relations found with her began and ended in their determination to think she had remained stationary at five years old. Of course Lady Mary, Governess-general, acted the most busy and prominent part. Lady Betty, having a good temper, a happy home, and in it some small business to mind, meddled only upon particular occasions.

Even here the dutchess frequently proved a safeguard. She had something about her which from the very beginning over-awed these good ladies; whom her cold dry resolute manner kept at so respectful a distance, that they durst only assail their niece sideways for any thing which her grace came forward to take upon herself. Her father and mother of whom they were afraid, were always in arms, ready to stand by her: and besides, wonderful as it may seem for persons of their birth, these Campbells looked up to dukes and dutchesses; an instinct strongest in Lady Greenwich, because her mind was the meanest of the three. In cases of great need then, *F.* might be pretty sure to find a tolerable shelter under the wing of her sister in law.

I come now to the aunt on the father's side, Lady Jane Scott. She was remarkably good-natured, very fond of her brother's children, and always as kind to *F.* as she had any means or power of being. But there are few families where an old maid of moderate fortune, keeping two women-servants, one man, and a sedan-chair, would have much influence; even supposing her descent from Solomon far more clearly traced than lady Jane's: and lady Greenwich held her cheap accordingly. In face, person, manner, and several little odd tricks and ways she exactly resembled her illegitimate brother, the Major; whom yet I believe she never beheld, naturally enough disliking to have any connection with the living proofs of her father's profligacy, especially those latest born. For you must know his grandson the duke and this son were just of an age.

You have surely seen in the world certain grave sober quiet women whom you would imagine nothing could tempt to leave the chimney-corner; who go about unmoved and seemingly never much entertained; yet who are constantly to be found in every scene promising amusement, because they have none but what they take in at their eyes and ears. Such was Lady Jane. Her love of public places, joined to her habitual taciturnity, made her an invaluable companion, or chaperon, to the *Exclusives* of that day, who could not appear at them alone and yet wanted to have all the talk and all the men to themselves. One may add too—who did not always want to have every thing they said repeated elsewhere. The Campbell sisterhood would have been evermore teazing her about "her fine friends" if she had in the least winced from their attacks; but she stood her ground with immoveable composure, and so regularly baffled their rude questions—"Where are you going now?"—and—"with whom?" —by this brief dry answer—"To a place—with a person"—that it grew a common phrase to say—"I shall go to-night to a place, with a person, like Lady Jane Scott"—

Next let me name an humble friend, an appendage to the House of Campbell, Miss, or Mrs, Cockburn, the same, who in token of her affection for *F.*, left you her bible and the only trinket of value she possessed. Mr Cockburn, her father, had been raised by John duke of Argyll, under whom he acted as a commissary, an army agent, or something of that kind, and was supposed so rich that his only daughter, an heiress-apparent, associated with his patron's children on a foot of no great inferiority. But he surprised his acquaintances by dying insolvent soon after the duke. The dutchess charitably maintained his widow, and on her death, being herself old and wanting a serviceable companion took the daughter to live with her.[1] When she too died, the four sisters agreed to give Miss Cockburn among them what was a gentlewoman's maintenance sixty years ago, a hundred pounds a year: to which Lady Greenwich and Lady Mary (now widows) added the farther boon of letting poor "*Miss Jenny*"—as they persisted in calling her when an old woman—reside with the one or the other during the summer months, in capacity of *Drummie*[2]—genuine and veritable drummie

[1] Lady Frances later arranged for a small pension for Miss Jane Cockburn, probably through the influence of Henry Dundas.

[2] Drummer lad, errand boy.

—to snuff the candles, ring the bell, go and come, and be their *souffre-douleur*, the lawful receptacle of all their complaints and ill-humours. Whether the footmen trod on her toes or not (according to the old Scotch lady's memorable speech) I cannot say; but they themselves did without mercy. In short she might have written the description of *Mrs Truman* in *The World*.[1] From her *F.* learned the faults found with her and the invectives uttered against her behind her back—sometimes most bitter when all outwardly wore the smoothest appearance. 'Though kindly meant, perhaps it was not wisely done to repeat them; but really fellow-sufferers, inhabiting the same house, must be more than human if they can altogether refrain from interchanging their lists of grievances; and the good woman had one merit which with you and me might cover greater sins, a sincere attachment to *F.*, whom she saw daily cause to admire.

To proceed with *F.*'s immediate connections, I pass over her second brother, Campbell Scott,[2] because I never heard one word about him, either from herself, or any other person; although he lived to be eighteen or nineteen. For the half-blood, Miss Townshend will come by and bye. Charles Townshend, the eldest son, was a stupid lout, confounding all one's ideas, when viewed as the offspring of so able a father. There seemed to be neither a particle of brain in his blockish head nor the seeds of a gentleman's character in his composition: yet, as when returned from travelling (for he was sent abroad and put in the army) he staid all day at home guzzling ale with the butler instead of mixing with his equals—which might have cost his lady-mother some money—she rejoiced in having a son free from the vices of the age; who frequented none of the wicked clubs and never went to the Dutchess of Devonshire's parties. His death however, a very shocking one, gave her no lasting or sensible concern. Being encamped at Cox Heath, he went to bed one night beastly drunk, and was found in his tent choaked and suffocated the next morning.[3]

[1] *The World*, No. 37 (13 September 1753), I, 219-226. The character of Mrs Truman is a widow forced to live as "humble companion" and "toad eater" to a wealthy woman who uses her as an unsalaried menial servant.

[2] (1747-1766).

[3] October 1782.

William, the youngest boy, promised better things. As a beautiful sprightly child, only six years old when his father died he was in *F.*'s eyes Mr Townshend's direct representative, his legacy, and became the very darling of her affectionate heart. So she spoiled him—said Lady Greenwich; and in future days whenever he committed any childish or youthful folly, the language was—"Aye! Mighty well—all Fra-ances's doing—Fra-ances spoiled him at first—she was his ruin, and I hope and trust she will live to taste the fruits of it"—Alas! 'Though she did not spoil him nor had it in her power, she lived to have many a pang on his account. He entered the naval service at the usual age, was upon the American station during the war, and behaved himself well; but when a youth of 17 or 18, unfortunately met with something that provoked him to fight a duel. No harm was done, and as the story told in his favour, it placed him upon somewhat higher ground than before. This, I am afraid, has much such an effect on a boy's mind in respect to quarrelling, as winning a large sum at first handling the dice-box would have with relation to gaming. It banishes wholesome apprehensions, and fixes the taste. William Townshend learned to pique himself on his high spirit, and grow jealous of affronts nobody designed to offer him. But both in the navy and army (for he quitted one service and went into the other) he maintained a good professional character, and at his return home after the peace, appeared a fine young man, handsome, sensible, gentleman-like, and if occasionally guilty of youthful follies, still disposed to keep company with people of fashion, his equals. This in Lady Greenwich's opinion was abominable dissipation, as it cost money—there lay the head and front of all offending—Shortly however there were signs of a lurking *oddity*; his propensity to take fire on slight provocations increased; he got into absurd quarrels and scrapes; at one time he formally announced to *F.* his intention to marry his cousin Miss *Townshend, soliciting her to obtain Lady Greenwich's consent: all which turned out a perfect vision, the young lady knowing nothing of the matter.

Ere long the tendency these whimsies betrayed, was fearfully

* Lord Townshend's daughter, afterwards Lady Elizabeth Loftus.

augmented by an accident that might have begotten it where it did not before exist, a fall from his horse* upon the pavement; at first supposed to have fractured his skull. After lying for some time in great danger, he recovered (one must say unfortunately) so far as to seem pretty well; but in a year or two grew more decidedly *odd*—sometimes extravagantly gay, wild with spirits; sometimes plunged in sullen alarming gloom; now intent on vindicating his injured honour from imaginary imputations; now dreaming of plots and conspiracies against his life. At length he began to scold and threaten passengers in the street for daring to look at him, and in short gave such glaring proofs of madness, that any mortal save his mother (under whose roof he was living all the while) would have taken measures to hinder his doing himself or others serious harm. But her mind was still looking out of the window, according to Marivaux; she went about complaining of him as if he had been accountable for his actions; and it never occurred to her even to consult a physician, until Mr Mackenzie, at whose table he had flown out and terrified the company, went to her and pressed it in strong terms. Then she wondered, disputed, strove to palliate the facts, hesitated, and delayed, 'till the poor man saved her all farther trouble by shooting himself through the head.[1] The coroner's inquest found abundant proofs to justify a verdict of insanity.

I have here hurried along the passages of years. By the time this catastrophe happened, *F.* had been in some degree prepared to expect it and as a wife and mother, possessed objects of nearer interest. Yet the shock was severe, and many an anxious hour had he cost her ere all her cares for him terminated thus sadly. Lady Greenwich got over the whole with much more ease; put on her mourning, sent her cards of thanks, and was just the same lady Greenwich as before. I am sure I could see no difference.

As money—money—has been repeatedly mentioned, let me explain how her love of it operated. Not in the common way,

* Of which *F.* nearly became an eye-witness; the horse passed her carriage in the street, so evidently running furiously away with his rider, that 'though unsuspecting who that was, she was frightened into hysterics.

[1] May 1789 at Richmond.

for she was saving and stingy without being oeconomical; and, since ignorant alike of business and household management, might be handsomely pillaged, provided the cheating went on at an even pace and kept the straight road. 'Though her weekly bills were ever so exhorbitant, she would sit still and accuse only the hard times: but if the expense of any one week was remarkable, the most cogent and satisfactory reasons for it's excess availed nothing. There were to be no *extras*; linen must not wear out nor the roof want repair; it put my lady in a rage. So the sheets fell to pieces and the house threatened to fall too, ere an extraordinary guinea could be wrested from her fist. Need I say it shut yet closer when the demand concerned other people's sheets and dwellings?

Miss Townshend comes next in order, but I will first say something of two persons, not *F.*'s relations, for whom she had a sister-like affection. The Montrose family were intimate with the Campbells, and as they passed their summers near Sudbrook, *F.* and their only daughter unavoidably became companions. Through *F.*'s means my sister—and I through hers—got acquainted with Lady Lucy.[1] We were both very partial to her, and she was very good to me; but I grant I must have taken my opinion of her upon trust from the two others, for I could not as yet have judged very clearly of characters. However she was undoubtedly both good and amiable; besides being very pretty; 'though not equal to Jane in Jane's best days.[2] She had an entertaining sort of dry humour which Jane has not; and apparently not the spirit of decision which Jane has: but then her life proved short, and nothing ever called upon her to act a leading part. In other respects they were amazingly similar considering the difference of their original habits. That Lady Lucy, by nature quiet and indolent, and accustomed from infancy to sit over the fire with a blind father and an infirm decrepid mother, should dislike the bustle of mixed company, could surprise nobody: the wonder

[1] Daughter of William, 2nd Duke of Montrose, married Archibald Lord Douglas June 1771 and died 13 February 1780.

[2] Lady Lucy's daughter, later stepdaughter of Frances, Lady Douglas, married Henry Lord Montagu of Ditton Park.

was that Jane, bred up amongst so many young people, inherited (as one would think) the love of retirement from a mother she never knew. I can hardly tell which of them would have been best pleased never to stir from Bothwell. Yet Lady Lucy, when in London, went about in a quiet way, and in particular seldom missed Almacks. "I do love this place"—she more than once said to my sister—"I thank it for all my happiness—I was sitting there, just there (pointing to a bench) when my dear Mr Douglas first came up to me and asked me to dance—Never shall I forget the delight of that evening!"—After their marriage, *F.*, whom they agreed in liking, was often their guest in Scotland, and they returned her visits at Dalkeith.

F.'s intimacy with the Dutchess of Portland was still closer and began much earlier. The Duke of Devonshire being the dearest friend of Lady Strafford, she coupled her niece and Lady Dorothy Cavendish as soon as they could be trusted to romp together without a nurse's superintendance. After his death his daughter lived with her aunt, Lady Walpole;[1] yet the tie remained unbroken, as three other ladies, Lady Strafford one of them, were requested by his will to assist in protecting her. At seventeen she married the Duke of Portland, and *F.* continually at her house, contracted habits of familiar acquaintance (to say the least) with all her relations and friends—Lady Fitzwilliam,[2] the Walpoles, Lady Spencer[3] etc etc. But there was no *reciprocity* to use a hard word. If you infer that *F.*'s friends must also have been acquainted with the Dutchess of Portland, you will mistake the matter widely. I have sometimes spent three successive evenings in her company, when *F.* was lying in or otherwise confined at home, yet, meeting her elsewhere on the fourth, felt uncertain whether her cold shy look permitted a curtsey or forbade it. You will conclude she did not like my face—and again be mistaken—for I dare affirm she neither liked nor disliked me, since my sister, a

[1] Rachel, wife of the 1st Earl of Orford.

[2] Formerly Lady Charlotte Ponsonby, daughter of the 2nd Earl of Bessborough, and cousin to the Duchess of Portland.

[3] Probably Georgiana, wife of the 1st Earl Spencer. Her daughter became Duchess of Devonshire and sister-in-law to the Duchess of Portland.

more popular person than I (as she well deserved to be) succeeded no better. Party might indeed set a black mark on us. We were Lord Bute's daughters; our brother in law Sir James Lowther[1] waged fierce election-war with the duke; and more than all, our mother was the bosom-friend of *his* mother,[2] whom he never loved. But Lady Lucy, Lady Pembroke,[3] and the rest of *F.*'s favourites were equally strangers to the Dutchess of Portland, and as far as I could observe, she seemed to be on distant formal terms with the Buccleuchs.

This chilling reserve did not proceed from pride for she had none; at least no regard to dignity. In days when few ladies ever walked in the streets at all, you saw her, a draggled figure, tramping along Pall-mall or Piccadilly arm in arm with some man, and without a servant. An odd contrast to the state and grandeur of her husband; although he controlled her in nothing. Luton was a show-place, and I remember their coming over to see it from Mr Plomer's in Hertfordshire. Mr Plomer drove her in a little chaise, the duke rode, and their escort consisted of—sixteen people on horseback. Nay, he carried down as large a retinue when hastily summoned to his mother's death-bed at Bulstrode,[4] thus with strange indelicacy dislodging her own attendants, and creating noise and bustle in a house where the silence of awe should have reigned, if not that of sorrow.

One evening at Mrs Delany's,[5] the constant meeting-place of the dowager Dutchess of Portland, my mother, and a few more old friends, Cecilia, then newly published, was talked over and the character of Delville senior pronounced exaggerated; for most of the party agreed that no such stiff personage, swelling with

[1] Later Earl of Lonsdale, husband of Mary, eldest daughter of John, 3rd Earl of Bute. He and the Duke of Portland were engaged in a bitter quarrel over fishery and property rights near Carlisle. In the general election of 1768 Lowther won a seat for Cumberland but was unseated by petition and the Duke's nominee returned in his place.

[2] Margaret, Duchess of Portland, died in 1785.

[3] Probably Elizabeth, wife of the 10th Earl of Pembroke.

[4] Seat of the dowager Duchess of Portland.

[5] Mary Granville Delaney.

family pride, existed in modern times.[1]—"I beg your pardon there", said the dutchess: "I know a Mr Delville; and it is my son the duke of Portland"—I took this for prejudice; they were each other's opposites, having no one taste or feeling in common, and he never paid her decent attention, 'though all he had to complain of, speaking fairly, was that she *lived* (to no very advanced age either) therefore kept him out of possession of *her* estate, for which his debts and his expensiveness made him openly impatient. Yet I heard him so highly extolled by most others, and *F.* especially had such an esteem for him, that I could not help being a believer in—"*Portland's mild worth*"—(see the Probationary Odes)[2] and supposing him peculiarly amiable and engaging when at his ease in his own family. And so by all accounts he was. Yet I must acknowledge that *F.*'s papers relative to the Wilsons contain a document which does not quite contradict the old Dutchess's assertion: the copy of *F.*'s own letter written to him as Lord Lieutenant of Ireland, to intreat he would do something for Mr Wilson. It was an irksome task certainly to plead for a person of whom she already thought but ill; and the consciousness of this might render it difficult to fall into her natural style. A *composition* might be necessary—but a composition it is, as studiously, and altogether as respectfully worded (your grace over and over) as if she had been addressing the king, or had never set her foot within his representative's doors. One must conclude that his manners, even in private, precluded any great familiarity, and that she was so used to the distance and deference required as to forget they had in them something not usually practiced elsewhere.

His Lord lieutenantcy,[3] brief as it was, proved a remarkable aera in the dutchess's life and seemed to work a change in her character; to which representation was so foreign, she had lived

[1] A proud aristocrat in Fanny Burney's *Cecilia* (1782), father of the man whom the heroine marries secretly. Chastened by the grievous illness of his son for his excessive pride and suspicions of the heroine, he finally accepts the marriage.

[2] Sir John Hawkins and J. Richardson, *Probationary Odes for the Laureatship, With a Preliminary Discourse* (London: Ridgeway, 1785).

[3] March–July, 1782.

so intirely in a coterie of her own, and so little in the great world, that people said—"Bless us! The dutchess of Portland lady-lieutenant! Why what will become of the Castle?" To their utter astonishment she made herself more popular with the Irish than any woman who ever filled the situation; throwing off her reserve as she would have dropped a shawl, and emerging all at once not merely a civil and attentive but a very gay lively person; and such she remained thenceforward. I am sorry to add that then, when she was two or three and thirty, unpleasant stories began to be spread about her. I hated the sound of them for *F.*'s sake—Have not you this feeling toward a friend's friend?—but I could not always avoid hearing it. My mother abhorred and discouraged scandal, but there were some who delighted all the more to ring it in our ears, and whom no check or contradiction could deter from retailing what the fine men—greater gossips than the most censorious old maids—said of the Dutchess of Portland's passion for this or that youth of nineteen. Whether *F.* had any notion of these odious reports is unknown to me. *A.*, who belonged to clubs, must have heard them. I do hope their sole foundation was the dutchess's careless disregard of appearances, and her foolishly liking to have at her command a troop of boys, proud to go and come on the great lady's errands. It was thus that Charles Greville, the handsomest and vainest of *woman-killers*, originally established himself in the house: in consequence of which the daughter, growing up, fell in love with him, and the parents, after some resistance, were forced to let her marry an impertinent puppy, by that time *un peu passé*, and not worth a single shilling, whom they had to maintain by quartering him upon the public in a patent-place.[1]

I hardly ever knew *F.* express such indignation as at the behaviour of this pair afterwards; she thought both showed great ingratitude to the dutchess, that the wife was wholly neglectful of her, and the husband treated her with downright insolence; while at the same time he paid assiduous court to the duke. She said too that Lady Charlotte seemed to seek out purposely the

[1] Lady Charlotte Bentinck married Charles Greville in 1793. He was the son of Mrs Fulke Greville, friend of Lady Frances. See notes 1 and 2, p. 78.

society her mother most disapproved, as if to show how little she minded her advice. Perhaps seeing her friend very unhappy on this account, and apprehending she might be made more so, contributed to reconcile *F.* herself to her death; which was sudden, caused by some affection of the heart, and which *F.* supported with more composure than I expected, being grieved and saddened, but not rendered ill by violent agitation. As I did not personally know the dutchess, I conceived it my duty to burn her letters unexamined, therefore from them I gained no farther information. The few I ventured to open were written in her childhood and like a child.

Now I proceed to Miss Townshend. She and I had one early game of romps together at Lady Strafford's; but my mother disliking childish intimacies we met no more 'till I was fifteen and she a year older. Then we rushed at once into a violent friendship. Friendship was my castle in the air. Never having had even a young acquaintance before, I resolved she should be my long wished for, favourite, confidential, inseparable friend, endowing her *gratis* with every quality requisite. This was purely the work of imagination; the heart had no share in it; and on looking back, I feel self-reproach for having too hastily given up all regard for her when in riper years I saw her as she was. But I am not writing my own history, so need not confess my own sins. Let that pass, along with many other things calling for repentance.

One of the delights of having a friend was to indulge vanity by showing her my verses—hitherto mostly kept to myself because laughed at and held cheap at home. Secrecy being no gift of hers (as I afterwards found) they were tossed about Lady Greenwich's house, and *F.* chanced to see some lines that pleased her so well she sent me an answer. From whom this came I could not at first conjecture; but I shall remember while I live the flutter of pride and pleasure I felt on discovering it. The most brilliant success never made any author half so happy. I read it again, and again, and again, morning, noon, and night, put it under my pillow, and carried it two years constantly in my pocket, as it's tattered condition (for I have it still) will attest. It opened a new world to me, recalled the agreeable vision once seen at my sisters' tea-table, and inspired not so much a wish as an *ambition* to know more of *F.*

This longing increased when Caroline was enrolled compleatly of the Grosvenor Square-society.[1] For her sake *F.*, the Dutchess, Lady Lucy, etc, took some notice of me: by degrees I began to compare the sense and spirit of their conversation with the insipidity of Miss Townshend's; and I learned with surprise and uneasiness that she behaved but ill to *F.*, on whom Lady Greenwich often made her a kind of spy. Indeed *F.* herself bade my sister give me a hint that whatever Miss Townshend could see, hear, gather, or guess, was sure to be carried post-haste to Lady Greenwich and construed in it's most literal sense, neither of them having the least comprehension of a joke. Poor *Hecate*,* as Lady Greenwich always called her, acted thus from levity and weakness alone: her character was *nothingly* rather than bad; not affectionate, but not spiteful or designing. However it rendered it essential to *F.*'s quiet to have as little to do with her as could consist with keeping upon friendly and good-humoured terms.

It would have been difficult to find a person who had not either more understanding than Miss Townshend, or less. There was in her a kind of half talent, a something, approaching to cleverness, yet ever stopping short of it, answerable to the French epithet *manqué*. She could write pretty good doggrel verses, she drew so nearly well you wondered she never rose to the pitch of drawing better; but to compleat any thing seemed beyond her powers. As for reasoning, reflection, judgement, discretion, accurate sense of right and wrong, they were far out of the question. Her mind had had no cultivation—at least since her father died. *F.* said he used to take more pains with her than are

* This name sprung from a jest of Mr Townshend's. "*My sweet witch*" was Lady Greenwich's fondling term—"Nay, said he, make it the first of witches, Hecate"—Observe that F. always said—"*Miss Townshend*"—Miss Townshend—"*Lady Frances*"—*Sister* never was nor had been in use between them, any more than mother and daughter between *F.* and Lady Greenwich.

[1] London home of the Duke of Buccleuch.

commonly bestowed upon a child so young. But I doubt whether the soil itself was susceptible of much improvement. Lady Greenwich let every weed grow there that would, and even took the trouble to plant and water one of the most preeminent.

To own the truth we at first met upon equal terms, for no head could be fuller of nonsense than mine: only our nonsense differed in kind. My romance was heroic and poetical, derived from Plutarch's lives on one hand, and Thomson's Seasons on the other; while her brains were stuffed—possessed—with lovers and conquests, and she expected that every thing wearing the form of man would hereafter come and die at her feet—Such things were new to my thoughts: however, knowing no better and seeing she was extremely pretty, I very innocently concluded it would be so. These notions of hers might be kept up by foolish maids and trashy novels, but I must say they owed their origin to Lady Greenwich herself, who ever since the poor girl could remember, had been talking to her of her transcendant beauty, and prognosticating it's triumphs over earls and dukes; pointing out one individual in particular as a lawful and almost certain prize—namely, the marquis of Graham.[1] His lordship knew his destiny betimes; consequently grew up with a fixed resolution seldom to perceive that he and Miss Townshend were in the same room.

What was worse, other men, without so good a reason for averting their eyes, neglected to use them. On our entering the gay world, it amazed me to find that she attracted little more admiration than myself. She had a very pretty face, but at that period there reigned an affected, sophisticated, Frenchified taste which would not give the prettiest face its due. "D— the young fellows!"—said Lord Lothian[2] (the late lord's father) "I ask them whether a woman's handsome, and they answer—'*she's vastly well dressed*'—" Miss Townshend was always vastly ill dressed through her mother's parsimony and her own aptitude to overturn drawers-full of frippery on her head. In figure too, a point then more minded than features or complexion, she fell woefully

[1] James, later 3rd Duke of Montrose. He was the brother of Lady Lucy, first wife of Archibald Lord Douglas.

[2] William, 5th Marquess of Lothian (1737-1815).

short of the mark; looking what the vulgar call *all of a heap* lumpish, bundling, and not perfectly straight.

Yet for some time extravagant hopes continued to flourish. Whenever they returned from an assembly, play, or opera, Lady Greenwich told her that such a young lord had gazed at her the whole evening, and such another made a push to hand her out, but was too late. Then followed calculations of their respective *worth* as matches.—"I would not have you accept A.B., he is in debt and the estate no great matter—C.D. might do better; I believe he may have five or six thousand a year—however be in no hurry, you should look higher still"—But the hour of waking from a dream must come at last; and when in process of years neither dukes, nor lords, nor yet simple esquires, rich or poor, presented themselves, both the ladies felt a disappointment which, souring upon their minds, put them out of humour with each other as well as with the world. Miss Townshend growing restless chagrined and peevish, and having neither principles of filial duty nor warmth of filial affection to restrain her began to treat her mother with such open insolence, that, conscience-struck the latter could not forbear saying to Mrs Cockburn—"Frances would not have used me thus—Frances never said such a word to me in her life—" Still, like bullies among men, she quailed before an audacious opponent: and in this state of discomfort they lived on, daily wrangling, pouting and growling, until Miss Townshend, now near three and twenty, went out one evening to drink tea with a couple of new friends, Sir James Cockburn's daughters, invented some pretext for leaving them early, was seen on Hay Hill stepping into a post-chaise with a gentleman, and came home no more. Next week she informed Lady Greenwich by letter that she had been long attached to Mr Wilson,[1] and presumed she would not refuse her in her present situation the certificate necessary to obtain a special license for their marriage. Meanwhile they invited the observation which people so situated should have sought to shun, by walking down St James's Street and going to the play in the green boxes.

The Almacks of that day, high in price, and managed by great

[1] Richard Wilson, of County Tyrone, Ireland.

(not *fine*) ladies admitted only the best company. The second best, backed by the indifferent, set up an opposition ball called the Festino in Hanover Square—by subscription, as they pretended but people easily got tickets at half a guinea for the night, and a shoal of men poured in, whose faces you saw nowhere else, and who startled you with the vulgar forwardness of their manners. Here it seems Miss Townshend was seen to dance with Mr Wilson; it could not be traced that they met above three times more; and in a fortnight the elopement took place. Where and how they had been so long previously acquainted they themselves only knew.

Farther researches ascertained that this Mr Wilson—whose name, when known, made nobody the wiser—was an Irishman, born to an inheritance of three hundred a year, but greatly in debt, of no profession, accounted a black-leg, and chiefly remarkable for having fought two or three duels. He soon showed his readiness to fight another. At Tunbridge-wells, where he and his bride chose to pass their honey-moon, a rose-coloured ribband tied about her lap-dog's neck caught the eye of fat Sir Watkin Williams,* as he waddled after them on the Pantiles. "Hey!" cried he "There's a fine collar indeed!"—"Sir!" demanded Wilson turning fiercely round—"Do you mean to affront me?" —"Affront *you*, Sir!" replied the fat gentleman astounded— "Bless me! I only said the lady's little dog had a fine pink ribband"—

Not many weeks elapsed before the bridegroom began investigating his wife's fortune, which to his grievous disappointment he found almost wholly dependant on her mother's pleasure. But Lady Greenwich after consulting with Mr Mackenzie consented to give her a maintenance and sent Wilson notice she should allow her two hundred pounds a year. Mr Coutts[1] delivered the message; whom he answered in these identical words—"Two hundred pounds?—Two hundred farthings!—It's a sum of money that I want—"

* The father of the present Sir Watkin, and twice as big: a Falstaff-kind of figure.

[1] Thomas Coutts, the banker.

In the full reign of powder and pomatum, when some great ball made one wish to be particularly well-dressed, and one had bespoken a first-rate French hairdresser for the purpose, it would sometimes happen that after waiting the live-long evening, one beheld one's fate sealed by the apparition of a dirty ill-looking fellow not to be touched with a pair of tongs, who announced himself Monsieur le Blanc's assistant (or journeyman) come in his stead. I never saw Mr Wilson without calling to mind my misadventures of this nature, for he had precisely the appearance of such a person. His conversation was bragging and his manner familiar and *aisy* like those of the Paddy in a farce. All his friends had ten thousand a year; he talked of his horses and his carriages, his estate and his interest; and when he addressed you as a lady, you could not help drawing back for fear he should give you a kiss.

I must acknowledge my firm persuasion that this adventurer was the very first man who ever furnished Miss Townshend with a fair opportunity of doing what she had long wished to do, and that poor *Love*, whose name is so often taken in vain, meddled no more in the transaction than if she had married the richest and most gouty old peer in the kingdom.—"Love!—A love-match truly!"—said *F.* at an after time, when particularly provoked by one of her letters—"God forbid I should not love Mr Douglas a thousand times better than ever she loved Mr Wilson"—

F. was in Scotland when the thing happened, and it shocked her not a little, for she could not be indifferent to the ruin of Charles Townshend's daughter. Besides, her kind and generous heart, overlooking past injuries, immediately put by self, and as if it had not been a just retribution, felt deeply for the mother thus repaid by the child she doated upon. She wrote to Lady Greenwich, striving to palliate the business as far as it's freshness would permit, and offering to come up directly, in case she could be of any use or comfort to her. Learning from Mrs Cockburn that this offer did seem to reach the heart and give unexpected pleasure she set out without delay, notwithstanding Lady Greenwich herself wrote in very kind terms to beg she would not leave Dalkeith or risk the fatigue of the journey; since on *her* part she could assure her she stood in no need of consolation "*Miss*

Townshend"—no longer Hecate—"Miss Townshend's behaviour had been so intolerable for a great while past, that the most obliging act in her power was taking herself away."

Lest you should suppose this bitterly said in the first throes of wounded affection writhing under what is "sharper than a serpent's tooth",[1] behold the account the late lord Sydney[2] once gave me of the scene he saw in Bouton Street, on his visit of condolence.—"When I heard the sad news," said he,—"poor Lady Greenwich's darling daughter gone off with an Irish blackguard—I thought myself in duty bound to call on my broken-hearted cousin; so I put on a sorrowful face and went. Well—there did I find her and half a dozen other beldames hard at it—tooth and nail—screaming politics for a wager, and abusing Charles Fox[3] and the duke of Richmond[4] 'till they foamed at the mouth. I durst not open my lips, for then I belonged to Opposition myself,—but I sate longing to ask them whether it was the duke of Richmond or Charles Fox who had been running away with their daughters?—"

Long before Miss Townshend's marriage our intimacy had died gently away, without any quarrel, or even any heart-burning. Mutually sensible that we did not suit one another, we each took our separate path, mine always drawing nearer and nearer to *F.*, with whom I gained some ground by means of the ladies Cunningham.[5] An alarm about the health of Lady Betty, who was thought to be going into a consumption, brought them suddenly up to London for advice—utter strangers in England, all helpless and forlorn, *F.* therefore put all her English friends in requisition to notice and protect them and wrote in the most earnest terms recommending them to my mother and my sister Caroline. These new acquaintances were real acquisitions. I found Lady Harriet a very charming, very superior woman, and

[1] *King Lear* I, iv, 288.

[2] Thomas, 1st Viscount Sydney, cousin to Charles Townshend.

[3] The leading and popular liberal Whig politician.

[4] Uncle of Fox, opponent of Chatham, and a liberal during the first part of his political career.

[5] Henrietta and Elizabeth, daughters of William, 12th Earl of Glencairn.

Lady Betty, 'though less captivating and not at all beautiful, still greatly to my taste. It was autumn, the town empty, and our leisure abundant, so during the six weeks they staid we saw them almost every day, making the time worth six months or six years of common London intercourse; and at their lodgings assembled several of *F.*'s own *set*—Lady Pembroke, Mrs Greville,[1] Mrs Crewe,[2] Lord William Gordon[3] continually—Not the dutchess of Portland—she might be in the country probably was—but I heard nothing of her.

Lord William I must enlarge upon, as the duke of Buccleuch's old friend, and the very life and soul of the Dalkeith Coterie in town and country. He was a character, an original; odd, clever, beyond measure entertaining; one of those people who appear to have bullied the world out of an unlimited license to say and do whatsoever they please. Upon any extraordinary speech or extravagant action, his friends coolly observed—"Ah! that is so like him!"—Others asked—"Will he never be shut up?"—alluding to the family malady[4]—but neither gave it a second thought. Wherever he gained a footing there he was master, sure to govern. You knew not how or why, but the whole family, men, women, children, dogs and cats obeyed him; nobody disputed his pleasure: nor could any body make a stand against him whom he disliked or had a mind to turn into ridicule. He set about it above board, visibly and audibly, with such force of humour, that, pleased or displeased, all held their sides except the victim. For instance, Mr Bowlby,[5] a shallow affected old coxcomb,—*but* the Dutchess's

[1] The former Frances Macartney, married Fulke Greville in 1748. She was author of the "Ode to Indifference" and other poems and godmother of Fanny Burney.

[2] Mrs Greville's daughter Frances Anne married John Crewe in 1766. He was created 1st Baron Crewe 1806.

[3] He caused a scandal in 1770 by eloping with Lady Sarah Bunbury. In 1781 he married Frances Shepherd, daughter of Viscount Irvine.

[4] Lord William's brother was Lord George Gordon, the eccentric instigator of the London riots in 1780, who was imprisoned for a libel on the Queen of France and died of jail fever.

[5] Mr Thomas Bowlby, husband of Lady Mary Brudenell, sister of George Duke of Montagu, the Duchess's father.

uncle—gave himself the air of sentimentally languishing for Lady Morton.[1] I have known Lord William sitting at supper in Grosvenor Square directly opposite to them, talk (more than half aloud) of Philander and Celia, Strephon and Chloris; expatiate—regardless of hush and fye from every side—upon faithful knights, and enamoured swains, and pastoral love, and platonic love, and the Lord knows how much more nonsense, 'till the whole company tired of hatching coughs and almost swallowing their handkerchiefs laughed out in chorus. The duke and dutchess declared it *too bad* but laughed like the rest. After one of these scenes, Lady Mary Bowlby, seriously incensed, would not speak to him. Then the joke was to entrap her into it against her will; watching her looks, and playing all sorts of monkey-tricks to extort a monosyllable by surprise.

He had no mean talent for a careless but spirited kind of poetry, and headed the band of rhymers at Dalkeith, where for one season it was almost a law that every inmate or visitor should attempt versifying. If any refractory person held out, something appeared written in his name, either comically like or comically unlike his usual language and opinions. Perhaps the folio volume of their works, dated 1775, may still lie in some drawer or cupboard there, 'though I have not seen it since my first visit in 1783. The chief performers, the two best hands, *F.* and Lord William, were by agreement, the nymph and swain of each other. He described her charms, deplored her cruelty, sighed and died, in stanzas often of great poetical merit. Abundance of wit flowed from her in answer. Would you believe that this, the strongest possible proof of indifference on both sides, gave many foolish wise mortals a notion she must be in love with him?—Even if I had not known her, the absurdity of supposing that any woman would amuse a mixed society with the expression of a real—and a *hopeless*—attachment (for so ran the story) must have struck me as most ridiculous. Yet I was forced to sit still and hear it gravely asserted. My poor sister Lonsdale (for one) would have gone to death upon the truth of it; and used to tell trumpery tattling people before my face how she pitied *F.*; for whom nevertheless

[1] Probably Katherine, wife of the 14th Earl of Morton.

she had a great regard—in her way—But her way was not mine. *F.* meanwhile, more diverted than disturbed, laughed both at the report and my anger.

Lady Courtown[1] (the mother) assured me that under all his fooleries Lord William was for a long time secretly pursuing the dutchess, and meant she should take to herself many of the passionate professions addressed, in verse and in seeming joke, to *F.* She even said she had seen him shed tears, or pretend to shed them, at his ill success. A decided libertine, I believe he was, likely to have few scruples about the sacredness of a friend's wife; but I am confident it never could have gone beyond cautious hints and dumb shows, probably altogether overlooked by her: a single word to the purpose, uttered outright, would have insured his being forthwith turned out of the house—as he had tact enough to know. Something like this happened at last; but very long afterwards after *F.*'s marriage and his own. His grace of Montagu,[2] ever subject to capricious dislikes—at least he kept his reasons for them (if he had any) to himself—took a sudden aversion to Lord William, nobody could conceive why; and not caring how it annoyed the duke and dutchess, treated him with such determined rudeness that he could not but quit the field. This *F.* herself told me on my asking her the cause of his unusual absence from Grosvenor Square. She added that it was the more difficult to guess what had offended the old gentleman, because 'till then he never would allow a fault to be found with lord William, let him play what pranks he pleased.

I resume the events of the year 1779, in the spring of which Miss Townshend married. *F.* hastened up to Lady Greenwich who received her with a show of cordial affection as new as gratifying, expressed the warmest gratitude for her visit, but insisted that she should return in six weeks to the place and party she had so kindly left on her account: for the Dalkeith family did not come to town that season. No good was yet to be done for the Wilsons, against whom not only lady Greenwich but the

[1] Mary, wife of the 2nd Earl of Courtown.

[2] George, 1st Duke of Montagu, father of Elizabeth, Duchess of Buccleuch.

other Waywards were all in full cry, multiplying invectives, and gathering stories, some true, and some false; most of them I am afraid, partly justified by pieces of folly not worth recording. These being early days and time required to let resentment grow calm, *F.* contenting herself with putting in a healing word whenever she saw it practicable went back to Scotland by the beginning of summer.

Late in that autumn died Lady Jane Scott. Her will divided her fortune between *F.* and the duke, bequeathing to *F.* in addition the place now yours,[1] which had been left her only a twelvemonth before by her own uncle Charles duke of Queensberry.* Mr Mackenzie and Lady Betty, who of all things wanted a villa in that neighbourhood, immediately desired to take it, and *F.* assented, but delayed coming up to settle this or any other business, because she had promised her friend Lady Lucy to nurse her in her approaching confinement at Bothwell. She went to her then as soon as your sister was born and staid with her above a month, finding her company even more prized than usual. Lady Lucy wanted chearing and support; her health seemed drooping without any particular complaint or symptom to create alarm. She recovered very slowly and remained weak and low-spirited. One day as *F.* was sitting beside her couch and the boys were at play on the floor, something led the conversation to second marriages—"If I should die—said Lady Lucy—I wish to God you and Mr Douglas would marry, for I am sure you would be kind to my poor children—Aye you may laugh; but I tell you once again I wish it"—At that instant he came in, and directly turning to him—"Do you hear? (repeated she) I have been saying so and so to Lady Frances"—"Well"—cried *F.* in her lively manner "what say you? Had not we better agree upon it?"—"By all means replied he taking the same tone "I think there cannot be a better scheme." And all three laughing it off as a jest, Lady Lucy let it

* It had belonged to Henry Boyle Lord Carleton, who left it to the Dutchess of Queensberry—according to the scandalous Chronicle, his daughter—Either she, as a wife, had no power to dispose of it, or exerted none; on her death it devolved of course to her husband.

[1] Douglas House, Petersham.

pass so, though she had probably spoken from an inward presentiment that her days were numbered. *A.* undoubtedly thought she had, when the following event made him sadly recall her words; for they sunk deep in his mind, as appeared from his repeating them afterwards to her mother.

The event alluded to, her death, happened within a very few weeks after *F.* had left her: left her with some anxiety, but not the least notion of immediate, or even decided danger. The shock was therefore terrible and the affliction one of the severest *F.* ever experienced. She came to town low and dejected in the spring (of 1780) to put the Mackenzies in possession of Petersham; which Lady Betty was so delighted to have, and have upon her own terms, for as little rent as she chose to pay, that she could not be fond enough of its owner. Whereby hangs a tale, to be remembered hereafter.

On the other side Lady Greenwich's unwonted fondness and good humour had very much subsided since their last meeting, and the stream seemed inclined to run in it's old channel. Now commenced what was not presently to end, a worry of worries about the Wilsons, who after a wandering twelvemonth spent here and there, were, as you may suppose, half starving, with a child near at hand to increase their distress. The all that *F.* could possibly supply for it's relief, 'though parted with at a great inconvenience to herself, was a mere feather in the scale. Where such people are concerned, you may apply to debts and difficulties Pope's simile of mountains

"Hills peep o'er hills and Alps on Alps arise"[1]

Pay one demand and up start twenty others. When they had thoroughly drained her purse, applications were still to be made to Lady Greenwich and old Lady Townshend,[2] and nobody but *F.* could be prevailed upon to make them. From *this* lady she got great civility, much palaver, and plenty of lies; from *that* as fierce an onset of anger and upbraiding as if she had been guilty of spoiling Mrs Wilson or had advised her to run away. Yet I

[1] *Essay on Criticism*, l. 232.

[2] Audrey, Lady Townshend, Mrs Wilson's grandmother.

must say Lady Greenwich did in the end give more than enough. The sums out of which she let the Wilsons either coax or frighten her, in driblets of a few hundreds at a time, amounted (first and last) to six or seven thousand pounds; which, if bestowed at once and secured by settlement, would have provided for her grand-children at this day; but, as it was, only encouraged Wilson's farther encroachments. Whether she parted with her money however or withheld it, the blame fell equally on *F.*, who, tired of the constant battles she had to fight, cast about to serve Mrs Wilson in a different and more effectual manner.

Henry Dundas,[1] not originally raised by the Duke's patronage, since his father was President, but very considerably indebted to it for his advancement, had now become Lord Advocate and so useful a member of the House of Commons as to have a good deal to say with Lord North. *F.*, whom he sometimes called upon in a morning, one day took courage and frankly told him the whole story, asking his assistance to obtain a pension for her half-sister, and, you may be sure, putting the love-match in the most excusable light it would bear. He entered warmly into her feelings promising to do all he could both with the minister and the minister's jackall or private secretary Mr Brummel, then a person of great importance, formerly a clerk (little above a servant) of Charles Townshend, to whose memory he professed some attachment. Any business that Dundas took up heartily was in excellent hands: he soon came to tell *F.* that Mrs Wilson had a pension of three hundred a year—"And I do declare (said she) he looked as happy as he made me"—Thereby will hang another tale.

The next point was to induce the Wilsons, in lieu of daudling about at water-drinking places, to go and live in Ireland, where £500 a year would maintain them respectably, and where, if you would believe him, he had one dear friend Attorney-general, and another something else as great. Paddy murmured extremely at being *banished* as he called it (to his own country!) it took *F.*'s

[1] Later Viscount Melville, leader of the Scottish interest in the House of Commons and a political ally of Pitt. His father, Robert Dundas of Arniston, the elder, was President of the Court of Session 1748-1753.

last guinea, and her endurance of many snubs, to enable them to move by discharging such debts as brooked no putting off; but go they did at last, furnished with a letter of recommendation from the duke to the Lord Lieutenant, his old acquaintance Lord Carlisle;[1] which by the bye it also cost *F.* very hard pleading to obtain. Lord Carlisle read the letter, received Wilson civilly, and promised to befriend him; with the usual *provisos*, the *whens* and *ifs* and *buts* of men in power. Thereupon the suitor held it expedient to show his face at the Castle on every levee-day; and it so fell out that on one his excellency passed him without speaking—an outrage, it should seem, which no man of honour could put up with. Accordingly Mr Wilson went home and in a spirited epistle told Lord Carlisle his full sense of it, freely releasing him from his conditional promises, but condescending to say that he nevertheless remained, with due respect to the representative of his sovereign, his Excellency's most obedient humble servant. Imagine *F.*'s dismay when she received a fair copy of this performance, together with a volume of explanations and justifications!—"See there!" cried her brother (to whom Lord Carlisle had sent the original) You would make me write—Why what could one do for this fellow if one were prime minister or Lord lieutenant oneself?—"

We have now entered upon the year 1781. Lady Greenwich growing more and more crabbed and uneasy to live with, *F.* began to revolve in her own mind the possibility of forming a small separate establishment. As there could be no doubt Lady Greenwich would rejoice to part with her, she thought it might be effected amicably: but whether her means would suffice for a house etc, was another consideration; indeed the chief; for the other's acquiescence in the scheme must depend mainly upon it's saving something, or at least costing nothing, to *her*. But nothing passed no steps were taken towards it, when *F.* set out on her famous tour to the Lakes;[2] previous to which it had been agreed between her and my sister, that the latter with Lord

[1] Frederick, 5th Earl of Carlisle, served as Lord Lieutenant of Ireland, November 1780 to April 1782.

[2] Lady Frances wrote a verse journal of her tour in 1781.

Portarlington, and Mrs Herbert,[1] who was to accompany them to Ireland, should visit Scotland in their way and meet her at Dalkeith. I shall not dwell on what they did and what they saw, though I had letters from some of the party by every post and I believe dreamed of them every night. The most interesting passage in your eyes will be, that calling at some house in Edinburgh they all unexpectedly met *A.*, whom *F.* had never seen since Lady Lucy's death. He was much affected; she so thoroughly overset as to remain nervous and unwell for two or three days.—"He has been here since"—wrote my sister from Dalkeith—"and seems to have recovered his affliction; 'though, to do him justice, not his spirits, for his manner is grown grave and quite altered"—

F.'s journey to Ireland followed next. The Portarlingtons pressed for a return of their visit, she hoped to patch up matters for the Wilsons, and the duke who had a mind to see that country and pass a few weeks with his friend Lord Carlisle, offered to escort her. There she spent the winter of 1782. On the great political revolution which then overthrew Lord North, after a reign of twelve years, the first act of the new Whig ministry was to recall lord Carlisle and appoint the duke of Portland in his place. Of course *F.* did not chuse to leave Dublin at the moment of her friend's arrival; therefore she let her brother return home alone, and considerably prolonged her stay: having too made intimacies with Lady Louisa Conolly[2] and others to whom she continued to be partial while she lived. No wonder she liked the Irish: their admiration of her rose to enthusiasm even from the first, and that their demonstrations of it did not diminish when they found on what terms she stood with their new Lady lieutenant it will not require much knowledge of the world to conclude. On the whole, this excursion cheered and strengthened her spirits so as to do her mind essential good. But you have read the journal she sent the dutchess of Buccleuch;[3] so without farther delay let us proceed to the momentous year 1783.

[1] Probably Elizabeth Sackville, daughter of Lord George Germain, who married in 1781 Henry Arthur Herbert of Muckross, Kerry.

[2] Daughter of the 2nd Duke of Richmond and wife of Mr Thomas Conolly.

[3] The manuscript is included in the Douglas Home papers, Box 191, Bundle 1.

After an absence of eighteen months, *F.* once more returned to Lady Greenwich's house, again revolving within herself the scheme of leaving it for one of her own, but hesitating and doubtful how to make such a proposal, when ere long a fairer prospect opened. *A.*, from the hour of his arrival in town to attend parliament became so assiduous a morning visitor, entered into such confidential conversations consulted her on so many points, called so often and staid so long, that it was impossible not to suspect he must have a particular meaning. One day as he rose to take his leave he paused, loitered, and asked her, not without some awkwardness, whether Lady Greenwich was scandalized at the frequency of his visits. Embarrassment is catching in these circumstances; she stammered out she hardly knew what, yes or no—"Well, said he, it is right she should be satisfied—by the way, the Dutchess of Montrose wants to speak to you; will you call on her to-morrow morning?"—Then shook hands and *exit*. With a degree of delicacy very uncommon he made *her*—lady Lucy's mother—his sole confidante and the bearer of his proposals, which she urged *F.* to accept in the most earnest manner, reminding her of what her friend had said at Bothwell, bidding her view it as a dying request, heaping praises on *A.*, and to conclude declaring she should go to her grave in peace if she could leave her grand-children under her care, but it would break her heart if she declined the charge. Tears and embraces followed on the poor old woman's part, severe nervous agitation on *F.*'s. As soon as she had given her consent, the blind duke was wheeled in to bless and call her his daughter: and Lord Graham,[1] when informed, protested nothing could have made him so happy.

As a fair set off against these unnatural sentiments of Lady Lucy's disregardful 'though nearest, friends, her cause (that is, the shameful affront to her memory) was zealously taken up by *F.*'s own kindred, the wayward sisters. (I need not now except Lady Strafford, for she was almost childish, and did not outlive your birth above a year) Lady Greenwich indeed, ever inclined to truckle to the worldly prosperous, professed herself overjoyed; nay produced three hundred pounds towards the trousseau, with

[1] James, brother of Lady Lucy, later 3rd Duke of Montrose.

a gracious apology (founded on the craving exactions of Wilson) for offering so little. Yet to her own click of dowagers she whispered that 'though delighted at dear Frances's wonderful good-luck, she owned she could not understand Mr Douglas's having so soon forgotten that charming woman—it was a foolish feeling for *her* to have, she knew—after all, she really believed him a worthy man—she trusted he and Frances would be very happy.

But Lady Betty and Lady Mary kept *their* foolish feelings under less controul; they openly winced at the common wishings of joy—"Yes, to be sure they were glad to see Frances settled—and settled in a style nobody could ever have expected—but when they remembered Lady Lucy—so lovely a creature—and so fond as she was of that man!—those sweet children too—Ah Poor dear woman. Little could she have imagined—No—fye! Don't talk of him—Not but that the dutchess of Montrose did quite right to put a good face upon it; only with such a dagger in her heart they wondered it was in her power—" My mother, who had always loved and admired *F.*, could hardly keep her temper with the old cats. She vowed they felt the same sort of envious spiteful grudge as a low tradesman would betray on seeing his former apprentice step into the lord mayor's coach. *F.*, born their vassal, bound to remain in subjection to them for life, a predestined old maid—she to break loose when nobody thought of it, set up for herself, and have a house, and place, and establishment shouldering their own!—It was a bolus that must have choked them but for the resource of pretending to hone and moan over Lady Lucy—whose spirit meantime, if permitted to look down, was rejoicing at the union she had, while on earth, thought so desirable.

The spring of this year being unusually fine and warm, *F.* and I often went to walk or sit for two or three hours in the retired woody part of Hyde Park, in order to hold private conferences on the new state of her affairs. Occasionally we took Archy and Charles[1] with us, turning them loose to play while we pursued our conversation. I remember one day as they were making ducks

[1] Sons of Archibald Douglas by his first wife.

and drakes with pebbles in the canal, and appealing to her which succeeded best, —"Oh! said she pointing to them, "you have little conception what a soft balmy feel it is that those creatures will belong to me, that they are mine!"—Another time Lady Charlotte Tufton[1] happening to stalk by—a person proverbially *the* old maid of quality, lawful representative of the corps—"Do you see that woman?" said *F.*—"For the greater part of my life I have been used to look at her as setting before my eyes what I was fated to be—I made the best of it; but, believe me, the prospect was no cheering one"—

When the match was declared and congratulation accepted, Lord William Gordon the first time he met *F.* took her aside to offer his, expressing his gladness in the strongest terms. "Whatever faults that man may have", said *F.* to me, "there is *heart* in him. You would not expect it perhaps, but I do assure you the tears came into his eyes as he was speaking." Very well. I repeated this to Mrs Herbert to soften her, for she did not love him because she thought he liked to have it supposed he had an affair with Lady Pembroke and laboured to give his intimacy with my lord that colour. She bounced up from her chair in a passion, sputtering so angrily she could scarce make herself understood. Would you know why? She had seen Lord William the day the news transpired, had run up to him eagerly with "Oh are not you so glad to hear it?" and got for answer a torrent of ridicule upon *A.* for marrying so ugly a woman, whose person he then diverted the company by describing!!!—Monstrous as this was, and natural as poor Mrs Herbert's rage, yet possibly he uttered his real sentiments to *F.* herself and *acted* the unfeeling brutal coxcomb through shame of avowing them in his character of fine gentleman. It does not justify *him* but I think it provoked me still more to hear that the duke played almost in the same key; that among his male friends he too could not forbear laughing, and wondering how it was possible for any body to marry his sister—Such are men—

You may believe I broiled and gulped in silence and was not so very kind a friend as to tell *F.* these particulars. She told me

[1] Daughter of the 7th Earl of Thanet.

one of a directly opposite nature, which yet gave her some disturbance. Mr Dundas called in Grosvenor Square, and catching the dutchess alone, said he came to pay her his compliments upon the occasion, and to beg she would assure *F.* nobody so ardently wished her happiness; but he must confess it was a severe blow to his own. He had been audacious enough to nourish distant hopes—In case Mr Pitt should take the helm, which now appeared likely, his engagements with him were such as to promise him a high situation, and he had secretly flattered himself that when so placed he might dare to come forward and sue for the hand of the person in the world he most valued and admired. —"Soh!" said *F.* "you see a woman little knows what she is about when she asks favours of a man. Truly after this I need not expect any more for the Wilsons. But who would have dreamed of such a thing?—Or how could it come into his head?—With a divorced wife, and daughters as big as myself!"—I saw pretty plainly that it appeared to her a scheme founded on ambition, and I am not sure but she thought his hopes *were* audacious, all things considered.[1]

We had more interesting subjects than these to discuss under the elms of Hyde Park. She dwelt much upon the character and disposition of *A.*, in whom she said she had nothing new to discover; all was known to her, all plain sailing. The having been an inmate of his house sometimes for weeks together and brought into close contact with him, had made her so thoroughly acquainted with his temper, principles and way of thinking on every point, and even with his peculiarities (though they were few) that she felt it a certainty she could suit herself to his humour. —"He is a safe man, added she, and what is more, a *comfortable* man—" She owned that the charge of Lady Lucy's children was most agreeable to her, and said she undertook it without apprehension, because she both loved children and understood them; had been used to all their little ways. But independant of this motive, she accepted him from a conviction of his being preferable as a husband to any other man she knew.

[1] Dundas was a suitor of Lady Louisa Stuart in 1785 and finally remarried in 1793. His second wife was Lady Jane Hope.

—"And yet"—continued she after this assertion—"and yet, my dear Lady Louisa I will now acknowledge to you that it is but very—*very* lately I *could* have consented—very lately that I could have so far overcome and stifled the miserable feelings of my heart; or indeed that it would have been honourable and right to marry at all with a heart so engrossed, a mind so bewildered"—I was amazed, thunderstruck—yet it darted such a ray of light upon several circumstances, that, after the first start of surprise, I wondered I had never had the sense to suspect it before. The inequality of her spirits which could not be disguised, the deep dejection which would succeed her greatest gayety, the efforts she often seemed making to employ and interest herself about odd trifles not worth her attention, the expressions she would drop (as if half in joke) fraught with some meaning more melancholy than met the ear—all this ought to have told me the tale beforehand—To give an instance; one morning when, sitting with us, she had been most transcendantly agreeable, flashing out brilliant wit, stringing together a thousand whimsical images, my mother quite charmed with her exclaimed—"What a happiness it is to have such an imagination as yours! You must enjoy a perpetual feast"—"Ah!" returned she—"So you may fancy, but I am afraid I know better. I often feel convinced I have two *Selves*: one of them rattles and laughs, and makes a noise, and would fain forget it is not alone—the other sits still, and says—Aye, aye! Chatter away, talk nonsense, do your utmost—but here am I all the while; don't hope you are ever to escape from ME"—

I now found she had been for many years—not less than twelve or fourteen—the best and fairest years of human life the prey of one of those fixed, deep-rooted, torturing passions, our being liable to which seems a part (and the worst part) of the evil entailed on woman by the condemnation of Eve. On woman I say, for man has so many means of bursting the chain that galls him, I doubt whether it ever takes so fast a hold. The fabulous vulture constantly gnawing, the giant vainly struggling to remove a mountain from his breast, are but emblems of a state of wretchedness, which Spencer's famous lines on the misery of pursueing court-favour for a livelihood would serve so well to describe, that I shall quote them—changing only a single word.

> "Full little knowest thou, that hast not tried,
> What hell it is in *loving* long to bide.
> To lose good days that might be better spent,
> To waste long nights in pensive discontent,
> To speed to-day, to be put back to-morrow,
> To feed on hope, to pine with fear and sorrow,
> To fret thy soul with crosses and with cares,
> To eat thy heart through comfortless despairs.[1]

"I will not tell you, said *F.*, that *he* ever felt what I did, nor perhaps is he capable of it; yet at one time I could not doubt that he was extremely inclined to make me his proposals, and would have done so on a very little encouragement. But no—Oh no, no!—I had just—only just enough of reason left to see that this must not be—that we must never marry—it would have been worse than madness to think of it—And I withstood the temptation like a famished wretch refraining from the food he knows to be mingled with poison."

'Though she entered into few details, and I durst not ask for more I clearly perceived that this invincible obstacle was the character of the person. She had suffered the torment of striving and striving without success to detach her affections from one whom her understanding and principles forbade her to approve, and would even have compelled her to reject. What the pangs of such a struggle must have been, what the strength of mind that gained such a victory, what the long, lingering after-pains I leave you to imagine. One particular only she mentioned, that in a conversation which passed between them, he had frankly avowed himself an unbeliever, almost to the extent of atheism. "I could hardly bear up 'till I got home, said she; then I gave way at once and cried all night with a sensation of despair not to be described"—

"No one (she continued) ever had a suspicion of my folly, but the dutchess of Portland, who knew me so well and with

[1] "Prosopopoeia: or Mother Hubbard's Tale", ll. 895-900 and 903-904.

whom I lived so much, it could hardly escape her observation. On her questioning me I owned she had guessed right, but told her it could never come to anything—"Well then replied she, we had better say no more about it; for I have a notion these things are only fostered and kept alive by talking of them." There it dropped and was never alluded to again by either. Considering how young we both were, did not this show some self-command?"—

She went on to say that very long after, indeed as late as in the summer of 1781, Lady Portarlington had also become acquainted with it. One night as they were driving home together from an Edinburgh-party something which casually passed in conversation struck a chord awakening such anguish that *F.* almost unconsciously let it escape her lips—"I know not what suddenly came over me, she said—I protest it was like a start of absolute frenzy" —When I spoke to my poor sister on the subject however, I saw she was far from having fathomed the depth of the wound. She owned that *F.*'s emotion at the moment of avowal had been almost terrifying, but yet talked of it as "*a fancy*" which of course must have evaporated away long ago: for her own feelings, 'though sufficiently keen and very tender, were all *domestic*, if I may so term it, and as Lady Louisa Atherley said of the dutchess of Buccleuch—"She did not understand *that sort of thing*"—

F. never gave either her or me the least clue to discover who the person was. I confess I had an eager desire to know; but so far from gratifying my curiosity, she besought me, as I loved her, to repress it, desist from enquiring, and forbear to form even a conjecture. The only thing she ever let fall which might have led to one, was a circumstance mentioned by chance in speaking of Mr Townshend. She had told him, she said, that she felt quite sure she should never be in love—the persuasion of most sensible young people before their hour is come—"Yes, you will," answered he gazing at her pensively—"Your brother will return from abroad, and amongst his young friends your eye will single out some man destined to be master of your fate"—"Good Heavens!" added she with energy, putting her hand to her forehead—"One would actually suppose he had been endowed with the spirit of prophecy"—Yet this in fact told me nothing: the duke might have had fifty friends in his youth whom I never saw or heard of. It only served to mark how early the mischief commenced, and how long it retained it's power.[1]

On her forbidding me to guess who it was—"At least said I, may not I guess who it is *not*, and lay a wager against Lord William Gordon?"—"Most safely indeed," returned she laughing; "I don't know but *that* might have been a worse scrape still, and let me tell you, no unlikely one to fall into. Lord William can make himself so agreeable that a woman altogether disengaged, seeing as much of him as I did would have run a great risk of being entrapped"—I now comprehended why she cared so little about the legend of her passion for him. In certain cases it is more than indifferent, it is comfortable to see the world go off upon a wrong scent; the gossips are welcome to propagate any story but the true one.

You must not imagine that, when the ice was once broken, the subject might be resumed at my pleasure, nor that *F.* expatiated upon it freely. Far from it: I never durst approach that ground un-invited, and she very seldom gave me an opportunity. "Trust me"—would she say—"the Misses whose attachments you hear so much of because they confide them to fifty dear friends, have in general not a conception of what *that pain* really is. Those who have the misfortune to know, are not so flippant about it. Deep and serious misery we may strive to fly from and forget, but we cannot dwell upon it with complacency as a pretty interesting thing"—"'Tis a disease"—she once exclaimed in the course of a conversation that did not concern herself—"I am sure of it—a positive disease"—

I suspect, dear Car, I am exciting in you no moderate degree of amazement. In former days I have secretly watched you and fancied I could discern that you looked back only to her marriage,

[1] In July 1781 Lady Portarlington conjectured that Lady Frances was "a little in love with" Lord Herbert, later the 11th Earl of Pembroke (*Gleanings From an Old Portfolio* I, 138). However, he was nine years younger than Lady Frances, and he traveled on the continent from late 1775 through mid 1780, so he is an unlikely candidate for the object of Lady Frances's passion.

which you supposed, not unjustly, must have been contracted through sober esteem and friendship. When time has poured it's oil on the waves of life, allayed every turbulent emotion, we are all unwilling that the young people who look up to us with some share of respect should know those long past weaknesses which we have learned to blush at. And this reluctance must be trebly strong between parent and child. Why then—the question asked once before recurs with still greater force—why then do I tell you what you perhaps never would have heard from her?—Because I cannot help thinking she would not have been hurt at the idea of your ultimately hearing it from me. Of YOUR hearing it—You alone of all her children ever felt the passion of real love, therefore to you it tells that she could fully enter into every thing you either suffered or enjoyed; and more especially that your marriage, far from disappointing any expectations of hers, gave her the satisfaction of seeing you attain what she, as well as yourself, regarded as the summit of earthly felicity.[1]

Oh Car, Car! How could you be blind enough to attribute the agony she fell into on first discovering the state of your affections to Scotus's want of rank and fortune? (Unless as far as his being poor precluded your union) No, it was the plague-spots that made her shudder, the tokens of that fearful malady which, she so well knew, might embitter your whole existence —These were her words to me at Bothwell—"When I found her peace was gone, her happiness destroyed, and I could do nothing to restore it, a hand of ice seemed to grasp my heart—" Here she burst into tears. But the instant she recovered "Come, come, said she (according to her system of never indulging in complaint) it will not do to talk of; let us think of something else. I must go to my plants etc" And she mentioned it no more.

You will sob over this passage, dearest Car. But set in opposition to it the hour when she gave Scotus your hand with a full conviction of his deserving and returning your love, and remember you may rest assured that *that* was the happiest of her whole life.

[1] Miss Caroline Lucy Douglas married Captain (later Admiral) George Scott, 27 October 1810.

We must resume matters of fact. The wedding took place on the first of May. As *A.* had no fixed home in or near London, it appeared natural that Petersham should be voluntarily resigned to the owner, or at least *lent* for the present emergency. But no such thing occurring to the tenants, *A.* took the only dwelling he could find, a most wretched one in Kew Lane where he & *F.* staid sweltering through part of a broiling summer until they set out for Scotland. You know, I believe, that I went down with them, and as it was my first flight from the nest you will conceive how the journey and every other novelty delighted me—Dalkeith and it's environs, Rosline castle, Hawthornden, Leith races, Edinburgh, Holyrood, Dr Robertson, Dr Blair, all the places and all the people I had been many a day longing to behold. But when the time drew near for proceeding to Bothwell, I perceived that the circumstances of *F.*'s last visit there began to weigh heavily on her spirits, and the image of lady Lucy to be uppermost in her mind. It was not her way often to weep or faint, yet 'though she did neither, her visible agitation as we approached the gate awed me into profound silence, and at last had the same effect upon *A.*, notwithstanding he struggled hard to keep up conversation. The children were brought as soon as we alighted; Jane's beauty, which was very remarkable, made us exclaim, and between that and her prattling about her doll, we should have weathered an awkward point, if the little boy, William, had not almost got the better of us all, by falling on his knees with great solemnity, to say—"Pray Mama, pray to God Almighty to bless me"—*F.*, catching him up, gave him a fervent kiss and neither she nor any body else uttered a syllable for the next five minutes.

In a few days all embarrassment wore off, painful recollections subsided, and *F.* enured herself to her situation as mistress of the house. The children were pleased, for they found her a capital playfellow; and I observed with a mixture of respect and wonder what use she made of her turn for little mechanical occupations—to speak French *comme elle en tiroit parti*—to serve the important end of keeping up good humour and companionship in a married life. At first sight, *A.*'s tastes certainly would not have appeared to correspond with hers; many of her pursuits and amusements he could not share; but what was of far greater consequence she could enter into all of his, excepting the sports of the field; and when they had spent a morning chearfully together in contriving a garden-seat, or tracing a gravel-walk, or even altering a set of shelves, she never suffered herself to regret that they had not a mutual enjoyment of Milton and Shakespeare. Her natural spirit of fairness and candour had always led her to consider even in her most indifferent acquaintance the good and agreeable qualities they possessed, without dwelling on those they wanted; to view each individual as standing by himself and entitled to have his own inclinations and his own character: therefore she was very unlikely to deviate from this custom where a husband was concerned, for whose plain sense and sterling virtues she had the highest value. It would have seemed to her as absurd to repine because he was not particularly fond of reading as to quarrel with an oak for bearing no roses.

But then—to carry on the metaphor—she had the wisdom to curb her own love of roses rather than give it it's former scope. I could see her take secret pains to bring her mind down to the level of common life, studiously weaning it from all that appertained to Rousseau's "*Monde idéal*", from whatever was high-flown, or purely sentimental and imaginative. You surely must recollect the expressive epithet she so often used—*unwholesome*—unwholesome talk, unwholesome reading etc—"All *that* is very pretty very interesting, but it is *unwholesome*"—would she say of a poem or a novel; nay sometimes of a conversation that trenched on the forbidden ground of dangerous refinement.

Yet all this, going on quietly, without the smallest apparent effort or self-denial, might have escaped an eye not intently watching her. Indeed such an air of ease comfort and gaiety reigned throughout the house, that one day, as we were walking by the river-side, I expressed the heart-felt satisfaction it gave me to be convinced she was happy. Nothing like a cloud passed over her brow, but she thought a minute before she answered "Yes, it is very true: I have a great deal to make me happy, and I am thankful for it—but cannot you conceive that one may have been *so* unhappy, and unhappy so long, as to deaden the faculty, take away the power of fully tasting happiness when all obstacles to its enjoyment are seemingly removed?"—"I can"—replied I; and there we dropped the discourse.

A fresh stimulus never felt before could alone re-establish the springs of the mind so as to give it back the power she thought lost for ever. This happened, she acknowledged, on her becoming a mother. At the moment of your birth she too was born again to a new existence.[1] New interests, feelings, pleasures and pains filled the void space, and if they could not obliterate the remembrance of the past, made it henceforth appear like a dream from which she had at last awakened. Yet (you will be surprised to hear it) the first prospect of such an event produced no particular gladness. It was quite unexpected; for she had been so accustomed to rank herself with middle aged women that 'though but three and thirty, she wondered and doubted as she might have done at fifty five. "This is altogether a new case do you see (she said) for which I was not prepared. I meant to devote myself intirely to these children here, to make them the sole object of my thoughts. Now all my wise plans and calculations are overset, for I begin to fear that this animal, who (people tell me) is certainly coming, may stand in the way of my doing my duty to them.—I know I am a weak unsteady creature, liable to be carried away by whatever takes a fast hold of the foolish part within me—so I have been pondering and pondering, and one resolution I have formed. It has always appeared to me that the most exquisite delight human nature is susceptible of, must be what a woman enjoys in suckling her own child. This I am determined to forego. I dare not indulge myself in it, lest it should create too much difference between these poor things and that creature which I already begin to feel I shall love far too fondly without any additional cause of endearance"—

The physical part of the business was unusually disagreeable: she suffered greatly from continual sickness, nervousness, and a general lowness of spirits; besides which she had, as you know, a constitutional horror of any thing like an operation (even of

[1] 16 February 1784.

being blooded) that increased the dread every woman must feel of what she is to go through in a labour. For the two last months also she lost her voice: but this complaint had not come on when I left her. It was settled that I should be carried home by Lady Betty and Mr Mackenzie, whom I met at Edinburgh, having gone to Dalkeith with *A.* and *F.* about the middle of October. Thus ended my pleasant excursion.

Before I went away some disturbances threatened to break out in the household, and they resolved to do on their return to England, what they had better have done the first minute it was thought of, or indeed what *A.* should have done as a preliminary step to his second marriage. It is almost as hazardous for a widower to let his first wife's servants remain about his children after he has taken a second, as for a prince to allow of his foreign bride's retaining near her the attendants she brings from her father's court. The removal may be a harsh proceeding, but it saves a great deal of pain in the end. In the former case the very virtues of the lower class prompt them to be inconceivably mischievous. If they were faithful and really loved the mother, they hold it almost a sacred duty to hate the stepmother, and it is well if they do not piously teach it the children as theirs. At best, by sighing and purring over them as objects of compassion, and dropping efficacious hints of what their late lady would or would not have thought proper, they put the present lady always in the wrong and contrive to hinder her having tolerably fair play. To be just however, good little Mrs Ireland Lady Lucy's own maid, was an exception. She had lived with her from her (Lady L.'s) infancy, she knew her regard for *F.*, she thought the dutchess of Montrose who promoted the match could not err; and more than all, she had a mild conciliating temper, disposed to keep the peace, whoever else might break it.

But there was a very different person to combat in the head-nurse, or *bonne*. I forget her name, for, Jane calling her *Mum*, we all called her so too. This lady of formidable mien and spirit, now for above three years in the habit of having no superior, ruled the nursery with a rod of iron, and was perfectly ready to rule the house likewise. At the very least she would let nobody in it, beginning with *F.*, interfere in her proper department. Even poor peaceable Mr Buckle[1] grew a little restive at a degree of impertinence he could hardly swallow as a gentleman, and represented that his pupils, now great boys, ought not to continue entirely under the controll of any woman-servant. Having bred them up, she had far more authority over them than he, counteracted him on every occasion, and took an especial pleasure in letting them see how cheap she held him. *F.* did certainly lean to his side, as she would equally have done had they been her own sons. Still she hushed all disputes as well as she could, thinking it not worth while to battle, because it was arranged to part with *Mum* on going to town. The boys would then go to school, Mrs Ireland (who had higher claims) agreed to take care of Jane, and thus *Mum* would have it in her power to make an honourable retreat, as only discharged because no longer wanted. But *Mum* on the contrary chose to fly out, abuse *F.* before the children, and say every thing that was false and malicious; by no means forgetting that she was persecuted by the cruel stepmother for her attachment to them, or that her poor dear late lady would as soon have parted with one of her eyes.

As far as Jane was concerned these insinuations did no harm, for she was scarce four years old and felt nothing for *Mum* but excessive fear, so rejoiced at a change that put her into the hands of the good-natured Mrs Ireland. Perhaps what *Mum*'s malignity threw out took more effect upon the brothers; Charles especially, who was no common boy, even then, in his ninth year. I own I thought him a most agreeable one; lively, active, intelligent, acute, with an understanding above his age; yet not at all pert or chattering. You saw he reasoned silently within himself, and had more power of thinking than many grown men and women. The drawbacks were a tinge of obstinacy and sometimes ('though rarely) of sullenness. At least Mr Buckle complained of it, for I cannot say I saw it, having nothing to do with his instruction or guidance. But the impressions once made on such characters are apt to be lasting, and perhaps *Mum* laid the foundation of much

[1] The tutor at Bothwell. Lady Portarlington suspected that he may have been fond of Lady Louisa Stuart. (See *Gleanings From an Old Portfolio*, II, 19.)

that one could wish otherwise in him, the chilling reserve etc, etc. Take this however as merely a conjecture of mine. For Archy, he was from the beginning the identical Archy you now behold him; only with higher animal spirits, because (if one durst say so) tops and marbles suited his taste better than any amusements he has met with since therefore kept him in good humour. I did not see him in the dismal hour of study. That was so hopelessly dismal, and the difference between the abilities and attainments of the two boys so great that it was thought best to separate them on their going to school, lest the younger brother should step at once to a higher form than the elder. Archy went to Eton, and Charles to Westminster where he remained until the death of William, who was there also.

When *A.* & *F.* came up to town, they took a furnished house in Stratford Place belonging to Sir George Yonge, who had in it a famous collection of pictures: so, as the lying-in tent was pitched in the best drawing-room, you were born under the shadow of two Salvator Rosas reckoned the finest that ever came to England; the one representing Diogenes flinging away his wooden cup as a superfluity on seeing a peasant catch water that fell from a rock in the palm of his hand; the other Heraclitus, the weeping philosopher, mourning over the general decay of all created things; the mouldering building, the withered flower, the dying animal, etc. Do you think it had a mysterious influence on your fate, and infused the black drop which, you say, makes your drawings dark-coloured, your music touching, and your style pathetic? It would not be an unpoetical system to lay down.

As soon as friends could be admitted I hastened to *F.*'s bed-side, and with great joy found she spoke audibly like her neighbours, the first attack of pain having restored her voice. But she had had a severe time. "You nasty wicked imp! said she, addressing *you*, "how odd it is that I should feel love for what has made me suffer so much!"—As you endeavoured to stretch out your little paws which the month-nurse kept constantly stroking in—"Look there now! cried *F.*, is not that exactly what we are all about throughout our whole lives; continually stretching and reaching at something, we hardly know what, and some other thing stronger than ourselves always pulling us back?"—The following day, instead of moralizing, she was fretting, with very great reason, against her maid—a Mrs Turner, whom you can hardly remember, for she went blind and retired upon a pension when you were but three or four years old. She had originally been placed about *F.* as a sort of governess, and, 'though of course not like the fine lady-governesses now current, had a gentlewoman's manners, and was far above the class of ordinary Abigails. "What do you think?" said F. to me—"Already—now—before this bundle of rags, this tiny bit of a thing, has opened it's eyes to daylight, the very first minute of its putting it's nose into the world, it is to be held up as an object of jealousy to the others—and by whom, of all people?—Why by *Her*!—that woman there!—would you believe it?—Jane was somehow mis-using a plaything, and what does Mrs Turner think fit to say to her in my own hearing?—"Oh fye Miss Douglas! If you do so, I will take it away, and *give it your sister*"—As *F.*'s anger never was very formidable, Mrs Turner stood by simpering, unconvinced of error, and quite ready to do the same thing over again. Of so little avail had it been to get rid of *Mum*, whose rancorous hatred itself could not have prompted any thing much more mischievous.—"*Dieu me garde de mes amis—pour mes ennemis, je m'en charge*"—[1]

It would be well if that excellent French proverb went no higher than the steward's room. Ere long Mrs Turner's superiors worked hard to put it on a level with any of Solomon's. I have told you what language the Campbells held upon *F.*'s marriage; Lady Betty perhaps secretly prompted by a lurking apprehension she was resolved not to betray, that it might lead sooner or later to her being turned out of Petersham. Accordingly it did so. *A.* could say nothing, while a lover, against the fears and delicacies that hindered *F.* from demanding possession; but when a husband, though desirous of living on friendly terms with all *F.*'s relations, he thought himself entitled to claim his own house and could not understand why the two things should be at all imcompatible. *F.* better acquainted with the *carte du pays* would

[1] Attributed variously to Voltaire or Maréchal Villars.

have delayed from sheer dread of the explosion she knew must follow.—Pshaw! What were they to wait for? What had they to fear?—*A.* with some difficulty consented that she should use her own soft words to prepare the way, instead of making solicitor write to solicitor at once: which however would have pleased Lady Betty no worse. A rough warning or a smooth was all one to her: The pleasant part of the story being, that she was not only as angry but as much astonished, as you would be if you got the same notice to quit your premises from Lady Dysart or Mr Hunt; seeming utterly to forget that the place was not her own property. She complained of *A.*'s having done the most unhandsome, unjust, unheard of thing that ever came into a man's head—and then the ingratitude of it!—*He* to dislodge *them* who had been his mother's friends, aye, and his own in adversity (Mr Mackenzie was a witness on his side in the Douglas cause[1])—Well! She should know what to think of him for the future—and of her kind niece too—Pretty behaviour Frances's truly!—It went so far that she would not speak to *A.* when she met him, and indeed showed him such gross incivility that he, ignorant of the Campbell-privileges, and not very patient of ill breeding, had a mind to get upon his high horse and ask "What right has Lady Betty to be rude to me?"—But *F.* patted him down, arguing between jest and earnest that it would do an old fool's nonsense a great deal too much honour to repay it with serious resentment.

My uncle, I am afraid, liked the act of ejectment no better than her ladyship; 'though he did not join in her invectives or seem to approve them. Some men make this convenient use of a foolish violent wife: a woman's prate is of no consequence, so letting her say what they could not well say themselves, they vent their wrath at second-hand; and a smile or a compassionate shrug saves the dignity of manhood harmless.

Next to the crime of taking away the place, came the crime of

[1] A prolonged legal contest (1761-1769) over the inheritance of the Douglas estates between Archibald Stewart, nephew of the 1st Duke of Douglas, and the Duke of Hamilton. The case was eventually decided in the House of Lords in favor of Mr Stewart, who assumed the surname of Douglas. See Preface pp. xvii-xx.

doing what they pleased with it afterwards; or, as a wit of a former age said of improvers—"carrying it a little about in a wheelbarrow"—The alterations they made were atrocious, they could not plant a tree or turn a walk uncriticised, and I thought I should never hear the last of four square hedges which, in Lady Betty's time, stood before the drawing-room windows. She lamented their removal as a kind of sacrilege and an affront to herself besides. Lady Greenwich and Lady Mary joined her in blaming these enormities; but they laid them on the shoulders of *F.* alone. Every thing wrong was solely her doing.

When A. began in earnest to build at Bothwell, he had to pull down most of the former house; therefore, 'till the new one was finished, *F.* perforce staid in London or at Petersham for want of a habitation in Scotland. He went down for a few weeks in the summer to hunt, transact business, or look after his workmen, but did not take her with him. If you had but heard the *howling* this raised over the memory of Lady Lucy!—"Ah! *She*, poor thing, was sometimes kept in Scotland all the year round—*She* who would have given the world to be more with her dear father and mother!—But there was no indulgence, no consideration for *her*—Frances may stay here and divert herself as much as she pleases—Frances can turn *A.* round her finger—Frances has everything all her own way—" And again there was the same curious contrast between the *howlers* and poor Lady Lucy's own family. The Dutchess of Montrose and Lord Graham going hand in hand with *F.* in whatever regarded the children and thinking she managed them to perfection; her good aunts finding fault and cavilling at every particular. *Mum* herself (so often mentioned) could not have taken more pains to inform Jane she was neglected and ill-used; fruitless pains luckily, for she did not listen: but the praises and caresses they lavished on her with an evident intention of mortifying *F.*, sometimes made a scene for a comedy.

Lady Betty's animosity gradually diminished when she had got another house at Petersham, and ceased to regret yours. Lady Mary's increased with the increasing sourness of age, the passion for ruling and the great lack of something to do. To pick quarrels with *F.*, and harangue by the hour on her errors and mistakes her omissions and commissions in the conduct of her own household grew really the business of Lady Mary's life. And an inveterate hatred of *you* commenced almost as soon as you could trot about and put two words together. You were—"an ugly child"—"a disagreeable child"—above all, "a spoiled child"—You have heard the famous speech she made to Lady Mary Stopford[1] that she could see in you the seeds of every vice; upon which Ly. Mary—(or Lady Courtown) who was recovering from a lying-in, and tired to death of the other Lady Mary's invectives, peremptorily bade her chuse another subject, for she would hear no more of the matter.

My task is now nearly ended; I approach the time of your own remembrance. Before I leave off however, I must tell you that I am persuaded *you* owe many disadvantages and vexations, many of the prejudices of the Dalkeithites against you, especially the established opinion of your having been *spoiled* (which was most unfounded) to the ceaseless assertions of that old woman. In this particular people differ. I suppose it comes from the spirit of contradiction being peculiarly strong in me, but if I perceive that any person is constantly and malignantly *pecked at*, it inclines me naturally to take that person's part without knowing any more about him, or ever having seen him in my life. Yet this is not the common way. One may say of censure as somebody did of flattery "lay on but enough and some of it will be sure to stick;" and indeed I have been tempted to think that constant repetition wears a hole in one's head, like the continual dropping of water on a stone. To reflect coolly—"who is it that says all this? what is my opinion of them? what credit would I (and do I) give them on other points?"—seems a process seldom followed. We rather reason thus—"there must be *some* ground for so much blame, and 'though to be sure Lady Mary Coke (or any other like her) rails too violently, perhaps there is *some* truth in this or that which she affirms." I only know that when I came to Dalkeith in the autumn of 1799, I often had occasion to say to

[1] Daughter of the 3rd Duke of Buccleuch, niece of Lady Douglas and cousin of Caroline Scott.

myself—"Sure Lady Mary & Lady Betty have dropped their mantles on their collaterals here"—I recognised the old spirit; 'though, I grant considerably softened; but it still delighted in finding fault.

I have but a few words more to say: The Wilsons continued to give *F.* annoyance at times, and as she could not now assist them herself, because her money was no longer her own, all she had formerly done went for nothing. No people ever were so inhumanly treated by all their great relations, no family in the world but Mrs Wilson's would have suffered her to remain in such a destitute condition etc etc etc—Meanwhile William Townshend died and left her and her children four thousand pounds, to be held in trust for them by *F.* and some man of business, together with two or three houses on Ham Common which he had at his disposal. By the want of a formality in his will, the legacy of £4000 proved void and devolved to his residuary legatees, who were *F.* and his cousin Lord Ferrars* of Chartley. The latter did not blush to take advantage of the mistake. He claimed *his* two thousand pounds but as you would expect, *F.*, with *A.*'s consent and full approbation disposed of hers according to William's manifest intention. Then died the old grandmother Lady Townshend, leaving Mrs Wilson two hundred pounds a year annuity; and what was more, her heir, Lord John Townshend, acting very differently from his brother, resigned to Mrs Wilson an estate of five hundred a year, which he found, on examining the papers, she had a legal claim to. I believe Wilson presently sold and made away with both estate and annuity. However that was, after all these considerable acquisitions, their outcries against Lady Greenwich grew louder than ever, and *F.* came in for no less a share of reproach, because, holding the £2000 as a trustee, she would not (*i.e.* could not) let them take possession of the principal. At length Mrs Wilson wrote to her, dilating on all their grievances, and pretty plainly intimating that if her mother and the rest of her relations persisted

* Lord Townshend's eldest son, afterwards created Earl of Leicester, on his father's death he became Marquis Townshend.

in their cruel and unnatural conduct towards her, it might drive her to follow her poor brother's example. This cool threat (for it was a threat) of suicide so provoked *F.*, as to draw from her the severest letter, but one of the best, she ever wrote in her life. There is a copy of it among her papers.

Before I finally conclude let me mention that those papers told me a circumstance of her history I never knew nor had any reason to suspect until I had the mournful office of examining them. In the year 1777 she received and rejected (but with extreme civility) a proposal of marriage from Keith Stewart,[1] Mr Stewart Mackenzie's father, with whom I did not even know she was acquainted. His letter is there, inclosed in one to the duke, whom he requests to deliver it or not, as he shall think proper. With these is put up the copy of her answer. Her silence on the subject by no means induced me to imagine him *the* person whom she refused to name. I rather supposed it was such a commonplace formal transaction that she dismissed it from her thoughts, said nothing of it at the time through an honourable motive, and afterwards almost forgot it had ever happened. He bore, to say truth, the character of minding his interest, and my own impression upon reading these letters was that he had aimed at making an advantageous match. Yet a singular thing occurred at the very time they lay before me. Mrs Stewart Mackenzie wrote me word that her husband had called at Bothwell (in 1818) and in giving her an account of his visit, protested he felt a lump in his throat when he entered the room where he had once seen *F.*, whom, she added, he always particularly admired: besides that she was an object of curiosity to him, *because of his father's having been so much attached to her*. I could not then talk easily of *F.* even on paper, so took no notice; but it is certainly very odd that he, who I believe lost his father in his infancy, should know this; and it proves there must have been some ground for the idea, 'though contrary to mine.

Here at last I make an end.

[1] Third son of the 6th Earl of Galloway and an admiral in the Royal Navy. He married in 1782.